MY ANGEL WILL GO BEFORE YOU

GEORGES HUBER

My Angel will go before you

With an introduction by

CARDINAL CHARLES JOURNET

A DIVISION OF THOMAS MORE PUBLISHING

Allen, Texas • Chicago, Illinois

FOUR COURTS PRESS • DUBLIN • IRELAND

This book, a translation by Michael Adams of *Mon ange
marchera devant toi,* is published by
Four Courts Press, Kill Lane, Blackrock, Co. Dublin
and
Christian Classics, a Division of Thomas More Publishing
200 East Bethany Drive, Allen, Texas 75002-3804.

Nihil obstat: Stephen J. Greene, censor deputatus.
Imprimi potest: Dermot, Archbishop of Dublin, 25 May 1983

ISBN 0-905127-72-2 Four Courts Press Edition
ISBN 0-87061-083-X Christian Classics Edition

1st printing 1983
2nd printing 1984
3rd printing 1988
4th printing 1992
5th printing 1995 (reset, with corrections)

Library of Congress Catalog Card Number 83-072016

The cover design by Jarlath Hayes incorporates a detail from
Follower of Andres del Verrocchio (*c.*1480),
Tobias and the Angel, reproduced by courtesy of the Trustees,
The National Gallery, London.

Printed by The Guernsey Press Co. Ltd.,
Guernsey, Channel Islands

*The Lord said to Moses, '. . . behold, I send an angel before you, to
guard you on the way and to bring you to the place which I have
prepared. Give heed to him and hearken to his voice, do not rebel
against him, for he will not pardon your transgressions; for my name is
in him. But if you hearken attentively to his voice and do all that I say,
then I will be an enemy to your enemies and an adversary to your
adversaries. When my angel goes before you . . . '* (Exodus 23:20-23).

Contents

Letter-Preface

I was very surprised to learn recently that you were going to bring out a book on angels. A journalist, even though he is well versed in theology—isn't that a rather daring subject for him to choose? Don't journalists always go where the wind blows? You could scarcely say the wind is blowing around angels these days.

My surprise grew as I read the book. It is indeed worthy of the angels; and it can stand up to criticism from any angle.

It addresses the ordinary person. It is not a theological treatise. It gives a direct answer to the sort of questions people are asking. Firstly, it does so in a very practical way, using arguments from authority: you allow the popes of our time to tell of their personal experience of angels. References and comparisons from daily life help, in the second place, to explore the truths the Church proposes.

Your book is very convincing. It combines a lively style with sound doctrine. You steer clear of legends and fairytales and try to present the angels as a very special, extraordinarily powerful world: to do this you use a great range of witnesses, covering all aspects of the subject.

As it turns out, your book is also addressed to the theologian. Here he will find, not only a great deal of information drawn from St Thomas Aquinas, but also references to modern theologians who have dealt with this subject. Of course, a technical discussion on angels was not your aim: I think it can be said that you have managed to find the middle ground between the theological treatise and a very general, 'pop', book.

I should like to finish by saying that your book really does speak to the people of our time. Even though it deals with a highly spiritual subject, modern man must realise that it is one which involves him and his problems.

Once they get over their initial surprise, those who read you will be delighted, for you have introduced them to the very wonderful and very real world of the angels. They will be grateful to you for strengthening their conviction that they have an angel as friend and companion wherever they go. And they will praise God for the wonders of his creation.

I thank you for writing this book and I wish it every success.

SIGHARD KLEINER
Abbot General of the Cistercians

Introduction

'Which is the more noble, I ask you—to talk about one's neighbour and the business of one's neighbour, and to be busy about the affairs of others, or to search into the affairs of the angels and those which are important to us personally?' St John Chrysostom, *Homilies on St John's Gospel*, 18.

They are *his* angels. 'When the Son of Man comes in his glory, and all the angels with him . . .' (Mt 25:31). They are his angels because he created them. At the very beginning, before man appeared on the scene, before the world was habitable, he created them out of nothing: 'in him all things were created, in heaven and on earth, visible and invisible, whether thrones or dominions or principalities or authorities—all things were created through him and from him' (Col 1:16). But later they will be *his* angels by a new title—which has a lot to do with us—when the only Son, who is in the bosom of the Father, after deciding to lower himself and become the Son of man, makes them the heralds of his plan of redemption: 'Are they not all ministering spirits sent forth to serve, for the sake of those who are to obtain salvation?' (Heb 1:14).

They first announce the mystery of salvation in a distant, indistinct way. Under the rule of the natural law it is they who close the gates of the garden of Paradise (Gen 3:24), who protect Lot (Gen 19), who save Hagar and her son in the wilderness (Gen 21:17), who stay Abraham's hand when it is about to kill his son Isaac (Gen 22:11), etc. Under the Mosaic Law, the Law itself is made known through their ministry (Acts 7:53; Gal 3:19; Heb 2:2) and they come to the aid of Elijah (I Kings 19:5), Isaiah (6:6), Ezekiel (40:2), Daniel (7:16) and others. And towards the end, it is an angel who prophesies to Zechariah the birth of John the Precursor and announces to the Virgin in Nazareth that 'You have found favour with God . . . and the power of the Most High will overshadow you' (Lk 1:30, 35).

The angels, then, are present during the long wait for the Incarnation, but who can express their awe when the moment finally comes when, 'bringing the first-born into the world', God says: 'Let all God's angels worship him' (Heb 1:6)? When Mary says, 'Let it be done to me according to your word', something altogether new happens in the history of mankind. Elizabeth, Simeon, the shepherds, the Magi: all in their turn will come to realise it; but at the very instant of the Incarnation the whole universe of angels is lit up; in their sky Christ shines out incomparably brighter than the Magi's star, and the angels celebrate in heaven the Word become man, in an act of thanksgiving whose echoes we hear, in our exile: 'Glory to God in the highest, and on earth peace among men with whom he is pleased' (Lk 2:14).

From this moment on we see them in position under the radiation of Jesus' human nature, a radiation which in some way they partake of. They protect him in his infancy (Mt 1:2), bring the good news to the shepherds (Lk 2:18), act as guides in the flight to Egypt, come and minister to Jesus after he is tempted (Mt 4:11), rejoice over the conversion of one sinner (Lk 15:10), are angered at bad example given to children: 'See that you do not despise one of these little ones; for I tell you that in heaven their angels always behold the face of my Father, who is in heaven' (Mt 18:10)— immortal words which associate forever in man's memory the innocence of children with the purity of angels. 'Their appearance is always a sign of God's direct and decisive intervention: a point where he no longer lets events follow their natural course, but instead takes matters in hand in a miraculous way, by means of the angels. Just as in the old Alliance Yahweh used them as instruments to guide his people, call his servants, reveal himself to his prophets, now they play a part in all the events of Jesus' life. Their role is particularly pronounced in the accounts of his birth and resurrection as in those scenes where we see Jesus dispute the decisive battles for the kingdom (the temptation in the desert, the agony in Gethsemani). . . . And in the same way, in the book of the Acts of the Apostles, they take an active part in the advance of the Gospel, thereby demonstrating the essential continuity which exists between the witness the apostles bore and the mission Jesus Christ fulfilled when he was on earth' (M. Bouttier).[1]

On the night on which he was betrayed, just one signal and they would have come to Jesus' aid: 'Do you think that I cannot appeal to my Father, and he will at once send me more than twelve legions of angels?' (Mt 26:53). When the end comes, 'the Son of man will send his angels, and they will gather out of his kingdom all causes of sin and all evildoers' (Mt 13:41).

'Thy will be done, on earth as it is in heaven' (Mt 6:10). The will of God is fulfilled first in heaven; it is later that it comes to be done on earth. The invisible creatures make it known to the visible ones. The former are given the power—and joy—of bringing help to the latter; the angels descend to men and where men dwell: 'Are they not all sent forth to serve, for the sake of those who are to obtain salvation?' (Heb 1:14).

Following a line of thought of Athenagoras and Origen, St Augustine will write: 'To the heavenly angels, who possess God in humility and serve him in blessedness, all material nature and all rational life are subject.'[2] We see how Christianity has replaced the old concept of a cosmos closed in on itself (St Thomas criticized Aristotle on these grounds) with a concept of a cosmos open to all the events of free will, a cosmos that can be shaped by the free intervention of angels and of men who, simply by letting causes play their part, without in any way undermining the laws of the universe or its determinism, suspend or modify their effects in particular instances. St Thomas does not confine himself to thinking of clearly miraculous interventions as possibly being the work of angels: he says that angels exercise a direct control (*immediatem praesidentiam*) over the lower material beings.[3] We might add that discoveries in the area of nuclear physics have the effect of opening up these horizons still further: they take us into a world which is still that of matter, but where matter is so indeterminate, at least by our measurements, that it becomes linked, by a certain suitability and affinity, to the invisible motions of the angels: thus, in some way, matter participates in the invisibility of spirit.

Jesus never ceases to speak to us of his angels.[4] The human soul, though it is not a pure spirit, is a spirit. Through its lower part it is open to the experience of material life, but through its higher part it is open to be visited by angels. In the silent and pre-conscious life of our mind, angels can sow suggestions which we are not aware of, in this way exerting a real influence on the comings and goings of our everyday life. At a basic stage—this is the most usual case—they do so in a very definite way; but what goes on in our conscience carries no clue at all as to where it originates: is it natural or supernatural? Who knows? 'What can we conclude', Maritain asks, 'except that we frequently take for a natural inspiration something which in fact comes from above? . . . When we get a sudden inspiration it may indeed have a purely natural origin. But probably, more frequently than we think, our guardian angel has whispered in our ear.'[5] At a second stage, 'the illumination and inspiration received are much stronger. In these cases they carry a mark (which we experience but which is ineffable) which distinguishes them from a purely natural process. A different sort of light is illuminating the soul. And then, when the light of inspiration is strong enough, the soul, with real conviction, adds faith to what has been revealed in that inspiration, especially (though not necessarily) when it has come in response to the prayer of a soul burning with faith and is in perfect continuity with a long experience of life of prayer.'[6] At a higher stage still, this prophetic light which one has experienced will carry the signature as it were of the blessed one (angel or glorified soul) from whom it comes: Joan of Arc actually recognised her voices.[7]

'And he said to him; "Truly, truly, I say to you, you will see heaven opened, and the angels of God ascending and descending upon the Son of man" ' (Jn 1:51). Exegetes have little comment to make on these words, but St Augustine meditated deeply upon their mysterious meaning.[8] They were addressed directly to Nathaniel, whom Jesus had just recognised as 'an Israelite indeed, in whom is no guile' (1:47). One needs a soul like Jacob's (to whom the angel would give the name Israel: Gen 32:29) to understand the dream at Bethel (28:10-19); a pure heart, to see the angels. But like so many other words of Jesus, these are addressed beyond those who heard him at the time, to people down the ages. Here is the question St Augustine asks: How can the angels 'ascend and descend on the Son of man'? Now he is reigning on high, in the heaven of his glory, at the right hand of the Father. How can he be at the same time down below, for the angels to be descending upon him? Only Jesus can answer a question like that. He has in fact answered it, St Augustine says, on the road to Damascus. A light flashed from heaven and a voice was heard: 'Saul, Saul, why do you persecute me?' (Acts 9:4). It is the same Jesus who is at one and the same time above and below. He is above in heaven, to enlighten us and intercede for us. He is below on the earth to be persecuted, in his Church, which is his Body (Eph 1:23). And in between this above and this below, the angels are continuously ascending and descending until the time of the Second Coming of the Lord.

CHARLES JOURNET

A dilemma

Quite some time ago two books came out, each in its own way inspired by concern for all the Churches, in this time of crisis of faith: *This we believe* by Cardinal G.M. Garrone, Archbishop of Toulouse and later a member of the Curia, and *But that I can't believe* by John Robinson, formerly Anglican Bishop of Woolwich and later a Cambridge don.

Both dealt with the question of angels. 'It is an understatement to say that the angels have gone out of style,' Cardinal Garrone wrote. 'We prefer not to think of them for fear of being confronted with a painful and insoluble dilemma. Either we must affirm with the Church the existence of these mysterious beings and thus find ourselves in the disagreeable company of the naive and the uninformed, or else frankly speak out against their existence and be in the equally unpleasant situation of rejecting the faith of the Church and the obvious meaning of the Gospels. The great majority, therefore, choose to express no opinion at all.' The cardinal pointed to two groups on either side of this 'centre': one made up of people who 'have learned to overcome their scruples' and are frequently counted with those who think and say they are intelligent. In the second group cluster 'what remains of the good people who still think with the Church, read the Gospel as it is written, and pray trustingly' to these invisible travelling companions given us by God.[1]

Dr John Robinson began his chapter on the angels with a quotation from the *New Christian* (a journal) which suggested it might be a good thing if angels disappeared completely from sermons, religious knowledge classes and the liturgy.

Dr Robinson argued that if we are sincere we must all admit we are of the same mind (as the *New Christian*): angels are just another piece of embroidery on the Gospel; rather than make our faith more realistic they make it more *unreal*, out of touch with reality.

In view of these conflicting opinions, where should a Catholic stand? Trusting in the traditional teaching of the Church, the integrity of the Gospel, will he keep on believing in the existence of these invisible companions of ours? Will he take them into account, rely upon them, on their active presence, in his Christian life? Or, rather, using a head-count as the criterion of truth, would he prefer to see angels excluded from sermons, catechisms and the liturgy? Should he act as if the angels are as fictitious as fairies, as unreal as Father Christmas?

For a first answer to these questions we shall look at the teaching and personal practice of popes of our time: Pius XI, Pius XII, John XXIII and Paul VI. Is it not the role of the bishops of Rome to confirm the faith of both pastors and laity, and build up the Church through their word and example? For Catholics, are they not the most authentic interpreters of Christian doctrine?

The answer the popes gave will tell us whether we can in good conscience join the crowd who deny the existence of angels or whether, instead, we should join that 'remnant of good people' which, though small in number, does believe with the Church that angels exist and are our guardians.

The Catechism of the Catholic Church

Published in an English version in 1994, the *Catechism of the Catholic Church* summarizes teaching on angels mainly in nos. 311, 327-30 and 332-6.

The existence of angels is a truth of faith, clearly enunciated in Scripture and Tradition (328). 'Angel' is the name of their office as servants and messengers of God (329). As purely *spiritual* creatures angels have intelligence and will; they are personal and immortal creatures, surpassing in perfection all visible creatures (330). Christ is the centre of the angelic world: they are *his* angels, created through and for him; he has made them messengers of his saving plan (331). The whole life of the Church benefits from their mysterious and powerful help (334), as the liturgy tells us. Beside each believer stands an angel as protector and shepherd leading him or her to eternal life (336).

I believe in angels

Pius XI confided to a group of visitors that every day, morning and evening, he prayed to his guardian angel. He added that, as the day went by, he used often renew this prayer, especially when things became difficult, as often happens in a pope's work.

'It is good for us to say this, also out of gratitude,' Pius XI went on. 'We have always seen ourselves as wonderfully helped by our guardian angel. Very often, we feel that he is here, close by, ready to help us.' Recalling what St Bernard said about our duty to respect, love and trust our guardian angels—exhortations the Church has included in the liturgy—Pius XI disclosed that as a young man he had the good fortune to take note of this advice; it made a deep impression on him. As his devotion to his guardian angel developed, 'it played a part in whatever good the pope has done throughout his life.'

Confessions of this sort may surprise some people; some may even find them odd. Here is Pius XI, who denounced Stalin and his persecutions, who confronted Hitler and resisted Mussolini, a pope as resolute as Gregory VII, actually relying on the help of his guardian angel and invoking him right through the day. Who would have believed it, if Pius had not reported it himself, in a public audience?[1]

In the same way as he frequently sought the aid of that invisible companion sent by God 'to guard him in all his ways'(cf. Ps 91:11), Pius XI often recommended this devotion to other people, especially to certain kinds of visitors—diplomats, missionaries, teachers, scouts. 'We always recommend this devotion to people in the front line. Often they feel they are on their own. That is the time to remember that they have a heavenly guide: God's angel is really watching over them. This thought will give them strength and confidence.'[2]

A marvellous secret

John XXIII revealed how Pius XI recommended devotion to the

guardian angels to the diplomatic representatives of the Holy See. Appointed apostolic visitor in Belgrade in 1925 and apostolic delegate in Turkey and Greece nine years later, Monsignor Angelo Roncalli lived for a long time in countries where Catholics were in a minority. The ecumenical spirit was not as prevalent then as it is now, and the Holy See did not enjoy the prestige it now has in those countries. Roncalli had a very delicate mission.

During one of his visits to the Vatican, Monsignor Roncalli was given 'a marvellous secret' by Pius XI, to help him in his work in the Balkans—active recourse to the angels. 'A source of continuous joy to those whom he protects,' the pope explained to his future successor, 'he smooths out difficulties and defeats opposition. Whenever we have to speak with someone who is rather closed to our argument and with whom therefore the conversation needs to be very persuasive, we go to our guardian angel. We recommend the matter to him. We ask him to take it up with the guardian angel of the person we have to see. And once the two angels establish an understanding, the pope's conversation with his visitor is much easier.'[3]

The private secretaries of Pius XI tell us more things about this great pope's friendly rapport with the angels. Cardinal Falconieri, for example, has described them as the pope's 'aides-de-camp': 'Pius XI had great devotion to the guardian angels. First to his own, then to the angels whom he knew were in charge of the various ecclesiastical positions and territories. Had he some delicate mission to perform he asked his angel to prepare the way and get the people concerned to be favourably disposed. And, in particularly difficult situations, he invoked the guardian angel of his interviewee, asking him to enlighten him and put him at ease. When he went to Milan as bishop in 1921, Monsignor Ratti knelt to kiss the ground the Lord had entrusted to him and invoked the protection of the angel of the diocese. He did the same thing, insofar as he could, when he arrived in Poland as apostolic visitor.'[4]

Another secretary, E. Pellegrinetti, later nuncio in Yugoslavia and a cardinal, told of how in the summer of 1918, just before the end of the first world war, when the German army was still occupying part of Poland, the recently arrived envoy one day visited the governor of Warsaw, General von Beseler. As was his custom on the eve of delicate meetings like this, Monsignor Ratti prayed fervently to our Lady of Good Counsel and the guardian angel of the person he was going to meet: by nationality Monsignor Ratti was from a country at war with Germany and he had no political or military weight to pull.

As things turned out, the apostolic visitor was right to be confident. Pellegrinetti, who was there, tells how Monsignor Ratti was so sincere, so careful and to the point in what he said, so grave in his tone of voice and spoke with such gentle conviction, that he won the respect of the General. While he did not get everything he wanted from the interview, he dispelled prejudice, reduced obstacles and obtained promises. He did well.[5]

Experiences like this leave a lasting impression on a person. And so when, as pope, he said good-bye to a prelate leaving on some mission he normally used these words from the liturgy: 'May the Lord be with you on your way, and may his angel accompany you.'[6]

A certain familiarity

Pius XII also spoke of the role of the angels in Christian life, but without confiding in people as Pius XI and John XXIII did.

We have two texts from Pius XII on the angels—a brief, but important, mention in an encyclical, and an address given a few days before his death. *Humanae generis*, which was issued during the Holy Year, 1950, warned bishops about certain errors which threatened to undermine the foundations of Catholic doctrine. Among these mistaken opinions, Pius XII, in 1950, denounced the views of those theologians who question whether 'the angels are personal beings'.[7]

To denounce this error in a solemn document means that the magisterium is implicitly stating that angels are indeed personal beings. It amounts to re-affirming the existence of angels as against those who call them in question, reduce them to the level of myth or make them out to be some sort of vague ethereal beings.

Pius XII's address, on 3 October 1958 to several hundred American tourists, is a real jewel of pastoral theology. It is quite short, but it is full of doctrine and can be applied in all sorts of ways. The pope encourages the faithful to 'have a certain familiarity' with the guardian angels. As was his style, he starts with things of everyday experience and bit by bit brings listeners to the reality of heaven. After evoking the beauties of the visible world—sea, sky, stars—which was so fresh in the pilgrims' memories after their journey, the pope reminds them that 'there also exists another world, an invisible world, but one as real' as our own. This invisible world, which is all around us, is peopled with angels. 'They were there in the cities you have visited, they were travelling with you.' Drawing on sacred scripture, the Fathers and the liturgy, the pope described the part the guardian angels played in their lives:

> Did Christ not say, speaking to little children, who were so loved by his pure and loving heart: 'Their angels always behold the face of my Father who is in heaven' (Mt 18:10). When children become adults, do their guardian angels abandon them? Not at all.
>
> The hymn at first vespers in yesterday's liturgy told us, 'Let us sing to the guardian angels of men, heavenly companions, given by the Father to our frail nature, lest we succumb to the enemies who threaten us.' This same thinking is to be found time and time again in the writings of the Fathers of the Church.
>
> Everyone, no matter how humble he may be, has angels to watch over him. They are heavenly, pure and splendid, and yet they have been given us to keep us company on our way: they have been given the task of keeping careful watch over you so that you do not become separated from Christ, their Lord.
>
> And not only do they want to protect you from the dangers which waylay you throughout your journey: they are actually by your side, helping your souls as you strive to go ever higher in your union with God through Christ.

Whereas we are inclined sometimes to limit the role of the guardian angels to that of defending and protecting us, especially as regards the material side of things, Pius XII goes much further, in keeping with all Christian tradition: our guardian angel, he says, actually promotes our spiritual improvement and helps develop our intimacy with God. He is a teacher of asceticism and mysticism, a guide who will lead us right to the summit.

Pius XII ends his address by exhorting the faithful to be on familiar terms, here and now, with their invisible travelling companions. 'We do not want to take our leave of you . . . without exhorting you to awaken, to revive, your sense of the invisible world which is all around us—because we look not to the things which are seen but to the things that are unseen (2 Cor 4:18)—and to have a certain familarity with the angels, who are forever solicitous for your salvation and your sanctification. If God wishes, you will spend a happy eternity with the angels: get to know them here, from now on.'[8]

'I talk to him often'

John XXIII was another pope who had a deep devotion to his guardian angel. One might say he practiced to perfection the advice of his predecessor gave those overseas visitors: 'Have a certain familiarity with the angels'. John XXIII's faith in the active and loving presence of his angel was such that, like Pius XI, what was invisible became in a way visible to the eyes of his faith.

The pope of *aggiornamento* often referred to angels in his addresses. He was noted for his simplicity and naturalness. He believed in the existence of guardian angels and in their role in relation to human beings, for all this is contained in God's revelation. There was no question about it. He did not argue. He did not complicate what was simple. He posed no questions which seemed inconsistent with revelation. God has spoken: that was enough for the common sense and strong faith of John XXIII. For Angelo Roncalli, the existence of angels was as certain a truth as that two and two are four, though the source of this truth is different from the source of mathematical certainty.

John XXIII believed in the existence of angels and he was happy to use opportunities to remind people of this reassuring truth. His words are instructive. In addition to exhorting his listeners to rely on their guardian angels, he sometimes spoke about the activities of these angels. Thus, in a radio message on 1 October 1961, he referred to the mysterious support the angels gave to priests' words to make them touch people's hearts: 'May the angels of God be the lovable heralds of our will . . . ; may the angels, present in every home, speak of our desire to bring about social concord, good morals, the practice of charity, peace among nations. May they encourage the faithful to pray for the Council.'[9]

Some months later, he was addressing priests, asking them to say the Breviary with increased fervour, to back up the Council. He suggested to them to remember the guardian angels: 'We particularly ask our guardian angel to deign to help us in our daily recitation of the holy Office, to help us say it worthily, attentively, devoutly, and in that way please God and do good to ourselves and the the souls of others.'[10]

But it was not only churchmen whom he reminded about the

active presence of the guardian angels. He liked to tell everyone about them, especially parents. Parents, he said, should teach their children that they are never alone, that they have an angel at their side, and show them how to have a trusting conversation with this angel.[11] 'Your guardian angel is a good adviser; he intercedes near God, on our behalf; he helps us in our needs; he protects us from dangers and accidents. The pope would like the faithful to feel the wonderful help the angels give.'[12]

Devotion to the guardian angels should occupy a key position among Christian devotions. 'We should never', John XXIII declared, evoking the scene of Bethlehem and the choirs of angels, 'we should never neglect having special devotion to the guardian angel; each of us has him beside him. It could be said that Bethlehem offers us a kind of synthesis of light: our Redeemer and Lord, Mary, who is his Mother and ours, St Joseph and the angels. There is where our supernatural life is nourished and reinforced.'[13]

So, it can be seen that John XXIII considered devotion to the angels an essential one for Christians. That is not very surprising for, as Cardinal Danièlou pointed out, 'the greatest among the saints and men of God, from St Augustine to John Henry Newman, have always lived on familiar terms with them.'[14]

Speaking to other people's guardian angels
Although it is good always and everywhere to cultivate the angels, there is a particular need to do so at the present time. The development of means of transport and all the speed and traffic of modern life: don't these imply an increase in risks, which call for more protection? By invoking the angels more fervently, John XXIII pointed out in an address on the highway code, we will get them 'to intervene to influence the minds and wills of people, and even the power of technology, when a misguided desire to compete or to break records might be a cause of disaster'. The leader of the Church wanted 'devotion to the guardian angels to increase. Each of us has his guardian angel, and each of us can speak to other people's guardian angels.'[15]

John XXIII was so convinced that angels were by our side that, when he looked at the great crowd of pilgrims and tourists in St Peter's Square on a Sunday, there to say the Angelus and receive the pope's blessing, he used also think of the equally numerous crowd of invisible guardian angels also present in the same square.[16] The same thing was true of St Francis de Sales, a saint beloved by John XXIII: before starting to preach he liked to look round at the people, to greet their guardian angels, invisibly present.

In a letter to Sister Angela Roncalli, a niece of John XXIII, when he was nuncio in France, he told her a little of his familiarity with angels. He wrote: 'Your name in religion, which echoes that of your uncle the bishop, and of your grand- father and your mother—the last two-mentioned already enjoying the visible company of the angels—should encourage you to have a close relationship with your angel guardian, and also with the guardian angels of the people you know and love, in the holy Church and in your congregation. It is consoling to feel this special guardian near us, this guide of our steps, this witness of our most intimate actions. I myself say the prayer, "Angel of God, my guardian dear" at least five times a day, and I often speak spiritually to him: it always gives me serenity and peace. When I have to visit someone important on business of the Holy See I ask my angel to come to an agreement with the angel of the other person so as to influence his attitude. This is a devotion which the Holy Father Pius XI, of blessed memory, often reminded me about, and I have found it very effective.'[17]

A former secretary to the pope, Monsignor Loris Capovilla, told me that this intimacy of John XXIII with the invisible world used to come out through expressions he would use, referring to particular visitors: 'My good angel has inspired me to do this; my good angel has inspired me to do that; my good angel woke me up this morning.'[18]

One last example of John XXIII's devotion is a little-known fact which has had an incalculable influence on the Church and indirectly on the world. John XXIII, in a private conversation with a Canadian bishop, attributed the idea of calling an ecumenical council to his guardian angel.

Did he have some vision? Of course not. He often stated publicly that he got the idea of a council while praying. In his conversation with the Canadian bishop he simply said that it was via his guardian angel that God gave him this inspiration.

No one should be surprised at God acting in this way, if he recalls the way things normally happen in the history of salvation: when he is communicating to us not quite a supernatural grace but an idea, a suggestion, an inspiration, God uses guardian angels as intermediaries. The angel exercizes a hidden influence on our faculties, says St Thomas:[19] thus God used angels to give his Law to Moses (Acts 1:53; Gal 3:19) and to inspire each of the prophets.[20]

God's associates in the government of the world

The solemn teaching of Paul VI crowns the testimony of his three predecessors. In his Creed at the close of the Year of Faith, the pope twice mentioned the angels: at the beginning, to state that they exist, and at the end, to recall their sharing in the government of the world.

'We believe in one only God, Father, Son and Holy Spirit, creator of things visible such as this world in which our transient life passes, of things invisible such as the pure spirits which are also called angels, and creator in each man of his spiritual and immortal soul.'[21]

Here I would like to explain something. The Creed in the Mass does not mention the angels; it refers to them only implicitly. It proclaims Christians' belief in 'one God, the Almighty maker of heaven and earth, of all that is, seen and unseen'. The Catechism of the Council of Trent explains that these words 'heaven and earth' should be understood as including everything that is contained in heaven and on earth—the sky, the sun and the other stars, the myriad angels; the mountains and valleys, the sea, all plants, animals and men. 'What we have said of the creation of the universe is to be understood as conveyed by the words *heaven* and *earth*, and is thus briefly set forth by the Prophet: "Thine are the heavens, and thine is the earth: the world and the fulness thereof thou has founded" (Ps 88:11). Still more briefly the Fathers of the Council of Nicea expressed this truth by adding in their creed these words: *of all things visible and invisible*. Whatever exists in the universe, whatever we confess to have been created by God, either falls under the senses and is included in the word *visible*, or is an object of mental perception and intelligence and is expressed by the word *invisible*.'[22]

At the end of his profession of faith Paul VI evokes those souls in 'the Church of Heaven' who see God as he is, . . .'where they also, in different degrees, are united with the holy angels in the divine rule exercized by Christ in glory': this expression echoes that of St Thomas Aquinas, who devotes the third section of the first part of the *Summa Theologiae* to this whole subject of God's government of the universe. Question 113 of this section deals with angels as guardians of men.[23]

As Paul VI's profession of faith emphasizes, the angels and the blessed in heaven are associated 'in different degrees' in God's government of the world. The elect intercede on men's behalf, while the guardian angels do not just pray for men but act on them. If the blessed intercede for those on earth, the angels both intercede and directly intervene: they are at the same time advocates on men's behalf in God's presence, and ministers of God towards men.

In November 1970, two years after the publication of the 'Creed of the People of God', Pope Paul VI, in the apostolic constitution *Laudis Canticum*, approved the new breviary, henceforth to be called the Liturgy of the Hours.

The reformed liturgy retains the feast of the Guardian Angels on 2 October. The earlier text is enriched by new material inspired by sacred Scripture and by tradition—particularly in the intercession prayers at Lauds and Vespers. For example: 'We praise you, most holy Father, for the angels, our companions: they guide us towards your kingdom'. Or again: 'You have entrusted to your angels the mission of guarding us: under their protection we will walk in peace and in joy.' 'You have charged your angels with announcing peace to men: may they inspire in the nations and in their leaders plans of peace.' 'You make angels your messengers, O God; with their help we proclaim your wonders.' We should remember that the angels are our travelling companions, who sow peace and joy, who support our prayer; they do so in their own way. They intervene even in politics, both domestic and foreign. This intervention in the world by angels should not in any way surprise a believer, for the Word of God is quite explicit: the guardian angels have been given the mission of guarding men in all their doings (cf. Ps 91:11), and therefore, faithful in their mission, 'they co-operate in all our good actions', as St Thomas Aquinas assures us (cf *Summa Theologiae*, I, q. 114, a. 3, ad 3).

From Paul VI's successor John Paul I, who was pope for only thirty days, we can give an interesting quotation about angels. Monsignor Albino Luciani was at one time Bishop of Vittorio-Veneto. During the Year of Faith (1967) he gave some lectures to his clergy about 'some contemporary errors to do with faith'. In response to requests from several priests he collected these talks in a small book now known as the 'Little Syllabus'.[24]

Among the dangerous tendencies and errors Bishop Luciani points to is denial of the personal existence of angels, good and bad.

'The angels', the future pope writes, 'are the "great strangers" in this time of "idolatry of the universe". Some Christians question whether in fact angels are personal beings at all; often they omit all mention of them. It would be timely, therefore, to speak much more often about the angels as ministers of Providence in the government of the cosmos and of mankind; in order to lead the faithful to develop an intimate relationship with them, as all the saints have done, from St Augustine to Newman.'[25]

Questioning whether in fact angels are personal beings: this denial reminds one of what Pius XII said in *Humani Generis* (see above, p. 16); 'ministers of Providence in the government of the world and of men': these words sum up very well the teaching of St Thomas (cf. *Summa Theologiae*, I, q. 112 and 113); leading people develop an intimate relationship with the angels: this is an objective the liturgy strives to teach us.

Pope John XXIII called for an increase in devotion to the guardian angels. It is in response to his call that I, a layman, have written this short book on the role of the guardian angels in everyday life.

As a journalist, up to my eyes in everyday affairs, I am quite aware of the extent to which people these days doubt the very existence of angels. I know very well that by speaking of their presence amid all the comings and goings of men (cf. Ps 91:11), I am liable to be regarded as naive or out of date. That doesn't bother me. I feel that the fact that this truth (which has been so vigorously emphasized by the Popes of our time) is being questioned, is just an additional reason for making known my own faith in the active presence of the guardian angels.

Would we cease to affirm the existence of the millions of stars in the sky just because some opinionated, short-sighted people denied they exist?

I have received encouragement to write these lines not only from priests and theologians but also from many lay people, who have read articles of mine on the subject, which have appeared in newspapers in many countries: if, as Christian doctrine says, the guardian angels have such an important role in everyday life, how is it that we hear them spoken about so rarely?

There may well be a profound connection between the contemporary crisis of faith and the decline of belief in angels.

In the Bible and the liturgy

To deny the angels,[1] writes a Christian philosopher in protest against the conspiracy of silence which affects them nowadays, amounts to tearing every second page out of the Bible . . . to say nothing of the Ritual.[2] 'From the angel of Paradise to the angel of the Apocalypse who swears that time has come to an end,' writes Paul Claudel, 'from the angel who appears to Manue to the one who enlightened Zechariah, from those who beat up Heliodorous to the angel who showed the way to the young Tobias, from the one who consoles Hagar to the one who sets St Peter free, every sacred narrative is criss-crossed by these wonderful brothers of ours, such good teachers, so full of compassion.'[3]

It is true: the whole Bible is marked by the mysterious presence of angels. 'Almost all the pages of the sacred books bear witness to the existence of angels and archangels', St Gregory the Great says in his homilies on the Gospels. Their presence is felt even when they do not visibly appear, as is the case in Genesis, the Book of Revelation, Tobias, Maccabees, in the Gospels and in the Acts of the Apostles.

'Father, how can I repay the young man who came with me?' young Tobias asks after the journey where he was helped so much by the Archangel Raphael. 'He has led me back to you safely, he cured my wife, he obtained the money for me from Gabael, he has filled my parents with joy, he protected me from the fish that was going to eat me, he has healed your blindness. How could I possibly repay him?' (Tob 12:2-3).

These words of young Tobias remind us very vividly of the material and spiritual benefits we get from our guardian angels. They also illustrate what it says in Ps 91 (11-13) which succinctly points to the role of these invisible guardians: 'He will give his angels charge of you to guard you in all your ways. On their hands they will bear you up, lest you dash your foot against a stone. You will tread on the lion and the adder, the young lion and the serpent you will trample under foot.'

Commenting on these words, a doctor of the Church, St Robert

24

Bellarmine, says that they can be taken in both a literal and a figurative sense. The guardian angels protect human beings from physical dangers and also from moral dangers. The Bible bears witness to this: they are indifferent to nothing which affects our lives; everything which in one way or another influences how we make our way to our eternal goal is of concern to the angels. In fact, they could make their own that saying of Terence, bringing it further: we are the friends of men and nothing which affects them is alien to us. The unleashing of the forces of nature, attacks by wild animals, human passions, intrigues, conspiracies, wars: everything can be the object of decisivie intervention by angels, once the eternal destiny of God's friends is at stake. In the Book of Tobias we see the Archangel Raphael, in the guise of a travelling companion, concern himself with curing the blindness of the older Tobias who had been the victim of the most banal of accidents: he is blinded by the droppings of sparrows. We hear Raphael himself give young Tobias advice on marriage morality and remind him of his duty to be grateful to God over and above any human affection or obligation (Tob 11:7).

Dying of thirst in the desert
Several times in the Old Testament we see angels providing people with the means of survival: an angel appears to Hagar and her son Ismael, who is dying of thirst in the desert, and causes water to spring up behind them (Gen 21:19). An angel woke up the prophet Elijah when he was lying, totally demoralized, under a broom tree. 'It is enough, now, O Lord, take away my life; for I am no better than my fathers.' The angel offered him a cake baked on hot stones, and a jar of water. Elijah ate and drank; then, with his strength restored, he had to walk forty days and forty nights to Horeb, the mountain of God (I Kg 19:4-8). And it was also an angel who took the prophet Habakkuk the food he had prepared for the reapers: in the wink of an eye he transported him from Judea to Babylon, to the edge of the lion-pit where another prophet was imprisoned: 'Daniel! Daniel! Take the dinner which God has sent you (Dan 14:32-36). And it was angels who for forty years provided the Jews with manna during their journey to the land of Canaan (Ex 16; Ps 78:25): every morning—except the Sabbath (for on the sixth day of the week a double ration was provided)—the angels performed their task and the Jews found the surface of the sand covered with manna, a food similar to coriander seed. In a particular way the

help of the angels is a feature of Jacob's stormy life. In flight from his brother Esau, he had a dream. He saw a ladder going up from the earth into heaven itself; angels of God were ascending and descending this ladder; meanwhile, the Lord comforted Jacob by promising him descendants as numerous as the sands of the desert and assuring him of his constant aid: 'I am with you and will keep you wherever you go, and will bring you back to this land' (Gen 28:11-15).

The angels appear to Jacob on his return journey, to confirm God's promise to help him when he meets Esau, whose resentment he fears (Gen 32).

Jacob got so much help from the angels during his life that, before his death, when blessing his sons, he will thank God for having led him, and his angel for having protected him from every kind of evil (Gen 48:15-16).

In the Old Testament angels often intervene to correct human beings: an angel appears to Hagar after she has fled into the desert because Sarah has dealt harshly with her and threatens her to make her return (Gen 16:9). An angel stays Abraham's arm, just as he is about to kill Isaac who is tied on the altar (Gen 22:12). An angel appears to dissuade Balaam from cursing the people of God (Num 22).

The etymology of the word *angel* shows that they are messengers. God sent an angel to announce to Abraham the birth of Isaac, as he would later send an angel to Zechariah to report the birth of John the Baptist. It is an angel who reveals to John what he is to proclaim.

They took him by the hand

When Abraham charged his servant with finding a wife for Isaac, he exhorted him to rely on his angel to cope with all the difficulties this mission involved. 'The Lord will send his angel with you and prosper your way . . .'(Gen 24:40). The father of Tobias had the same kind of faith when he consoled his wife after their son had departed: 'Do not worry, my sister; he will return safe and sound, and your eyes will see him. For a good angel will go with him; his journey will be successful, and he will come back safe and sound' (Tob 5:20-21).

To safeguard their protégés, the angels brook no resistance. Thus, when Lot and his family were in two minds about leaving Sodom before it would be destroyed by fire, two angels 'seized him and his wife and his two daughters by the hand, the Lord being merciful to him, and they brought him forth and set him outside the city' (Gen 19:16). It was an angel who closed the mouths of the hungry lions when King Darius had thrown Daniel into the lion-pit: 'My God sent his angel and shut the lions' mouths, and they have not hurt me, because I was found blameless before him . . .' (Dan 6:22).

The angels are seen to have had similar power over the forces of nature when they free the young men whom King Nebuchadnezzar has thrown into the fiery furnace for refusing to worship the gold idol. Shadrach, Meshach and Abednego were tied and thrown into the furnace which had been heated to seven times its normal temperature. The three young Hebrews, who had placed their trust in the Lord, walked unharmed amid the flames; meanwhile the king's servants kept feeding the fire with pitch, tow and brush. The flames arose forty-nine cubits above the furnace and burned the Chaldeans who were too close to it. 'The angel of the Lord came down into the furnace with Azariah (Shadrach) and his companions, and drove the fiery flame out of the furnace, and made in the midst of the furnace like a moist whistling wind, so that the fire did not touch them at all or hurt them or trouble them.' Bowled over by such a clear intervention by God through the ministry of angels, the three young men began to glorify God in a song which the Church has included in her liturgy and recommends as a thanksgiving prayer after Communion.

The king, who saw this miracle happen, recognized the angel in the furnace, alongside the three Hebrews: 'I see four men loose, walking in the midst of the fire, and they are not hurt; and the appearance of the fourth is like a son of the gods . . . . Blessed be the God of Shadrach, Meshach and Abednego, who has sent his angel and delivered his servants who trusted him, and set at nought the king's command, and yielded up their bodies rather than serve and worship any god except their own God.'

How wise and upright this pagan monarch was: he is impressed by the superhuman majesty of the angel and he pays homage to the young men's spirit of faith and to their fidelity to God. So impressed is he by the miracle that he even promises, 'I make a decree: any people, nation, or language that speaks anything against the God of Shadrach, Meshach, and Abednego shall be torn limb from limb, and their houses laid in ruins; for there is no other God who is able to deliver in this way' (Dan 3).

But especially when the existence of the chosen people is at risk does God send his angels: docile in listening to his orders, they are as prompt in carrying them out (cf. Ps 103:21). Are the angels 'not all ministering spirits sent forth to serve, for the sake of those who are to obtain salvation?' (Heb 1:14). Pharaoh did everything he could to prevent the Israelites from leaving Egypt and returning to the land of Canaan. To break the King's opposition and set his people free, God inflicts a huge punishment: one night, by the hand of his angel, he kills all the first-born men and animals.

Later, by means of an angel God leads the Hebrews over a period of forty years, through thousands of difficulties, from the banks of the Nile to the Promised Land. To prevent the Egyptian army attacking the Israelite rearguard, he put darkness between the two armies (Jos 24:7).

During the day, the angel spread a huge cloud over the Israelites to protect them from the sun and at night he lit a column of fire to show them the way. This angelic help was what led the Israelites to be docile. 'Behold, I send an angel before you, to guard you on the way and to bring you to the place which I have prepared. Give heed to him and hearken to his voice, do not rebel against him . . . if you hearken attentively to his voice and do all that I say, then I will be an enemy to your enemies, and an adversary to your adversaries. When my angel goes before you . . .'(Ex 23:20-23).

They saw a horseman appear
An angel comforted Josuah outside Jericho, promising him victory, just as later an angel will train Gideon and help him to organize his victorious campaign against Midian.

The aid of the angels is seen in the story of the Maccabees, those Jews who rose up against the Syrian occupation and defended the cult of the true God in the face of idolatry.

Beaten before by the Jews, the Syrian general, Timothy, prepares for a war of vengeance, with a tremendous army of mercenaries and a large contingent of Asian cavalry. Before entering into battle, Judas Maccabeus and his companions set to praying. They beg God to be an enemy to their enemies, an adversary to their adversaries, as he had promised (Ex 23:22). In the thick of the battle the Syrians see five resplendent men appear in the sky, riding on horses with golden bridles, coming to lead the Jews. They surround Maccabeus and, protecting him with their own armour

MY ANGEL

and weapons, they keep him from being wounded. 'They showered arrows and thunderbolts upon the enemy so that, confused and blinded, they were thrown into disorder and cut to pieces' (2 Mac 10). Angered by the defeat of Timothy, Lysias, the chief minister of the king of Syria, gathers a new army of 80,000 and a troop of mighty elephants. The Jews begin to panic: 'all the people, with lamentations and tears, besought the Lord to send a good angel to save Israel.' Judas Maccabeus begins to march into battle. 'And to these, while they were still near Jerusalem, a horseman appeared at their head, clothed in white and brandishing weapons of gold.' Comforted by the presence of the angel, the Jewish soldiers, scripture says, were 'ready to assail not only men but the wildest beasts or walls of iron' (2 Mac 11:9).[4] They fell like lions on the Syrians and came away victorious: Lysias, 'as he was not without intelligence', reflected on his defeat. He realized that help from God had made the Jews invincible: the Almighty God had fought on their side (2 Mac 11).

Some years later, there was a new Syrian campaign against the Jews, led by Nicanor. The Jews invoked the help of the angel of the Lord: the help came and again they were victorious.

During the period when the Syrians occupied Judea, an angel intervened in a very spectacular way on the day when Heliodorus, the chief minister of King Seleucus IV, tried to lay hands on the Temple treasure. All Jerusalem was in consternation, yet still Heliodorus persisted and went right into the treasure chamber. Then the Lord of spirits showed his absolute power: there appeared to them a magnificently caparisoned horse, with a rider of frightening mien, who rushed furiously at Heliodorus and struck at him with his front hooves. Two other young men also appeared, handsome, strong, majestic, magnificently dressed, and scourged him continuously. Thus it was that three angels saved the Temple treasure (2 Mac 3).

Coming to our aid
The interventions by angels in the New Testament are more familiar to us.

Angels announce the Incarnation of the Word to Mary: they tell the shepherds of his birth, the holy women of his resurrection, the apostles of his triumphant coming at the end of time. Angels minister to Jesus after he is tempted in the desert, and an angel comforts him in the garden of Gethsemani. Jesus himself spoke about the angels on a number of occasions: the angels of children, who both contemplate the face of God and act as children's guardians; the joy of angels at the conversion of sinners; the legion of angels who could defend him when he is arrested; the myriad angels who accompany Christ the Judge at the end of time; angels who gather the elect and keep back the wicked; the vocation of human beings called to share in heaven the life that angels enjoy.

The role of angels in the life of St Joseph is quite pronounced. They appear to him in dreams at decisive points in his life, getting him to take Mary as his wife, to fly to Egypt in order to save the child from Herod's fury, and, finally, after the King's death, to return first to the land of Israel and then to Nazareth.

Angels intervene in a visible way in the beginnings of the Church: they set free the apostles when they are imprisoned by the Jews, and later they free Peter, when he is arrested a second time. They guide the ministry of the apostles and their helpers, in the direction of the gentiles. An angel puts Peter in contact with Cornelius, a Roman centurion of the Caesarean garrison, to baptize him and his family. An angel tells Philip the deacon, en route from Jerusalem to Gaza, to initiate an African into the faith, a minister of the Kandake of Ethiopia. And it is an angel, in Troas, in the guise of a Macedonian, who appears to Paul by night and begs him to cross over and bring the gospel to Europe: 'Come over into Macedonia, and help us.'[5]

Expelling an invader
Precisely because, along with the inspired biblical writers and the entire Christian tradition, she sees angels as born protectors, counsellors and guides of mankind as it makes its way to an eternal destiny, the Church, in her liturgy, entrusts her children to the care of the angels. This guardianship of theirs is not something added on to the structures of the economy of salvation; it is one of its essential elements. The ministry of angels is the way that God, the source of all good, normally enlightens men.

Night Prayer in the liturgy begins with a reminder of the devil, who roams like a roaring lion seeking whom he may devour; it closes with an invocation to the guardian angels, calling on them to counteract the snares of the devil and dwell in the house of men to guard them in peace.

There are many—and perhaps little known—passages of the Gospel which show Christ as a leader bent on reconquering a land invaded by his enemy—Satan, the prince of this world. And there are as many prayers in the Ritual which pray God to cast down devils and replace their tyrannical influence over men and material things with the liberating presence of the angels.

For example, when he blesses a stable, the priest asks the Lord to protect the place from the wickedness and snares of the devil. When she blesses sick animals, the Church prays that all influence exercized by the power of Satan over them be cast out. When the fields are blessed, she asks God to expel the demons and send the angels: the evil angels are put to flight, the good angels take over.

'Deign to send your good angel from heaven to guard and protect this bridge, and all who cross it': this is the Church's prayer at the blessing of a bridge. Like a military leader, she positions a warrior angel to protect those who travel by it.

'Lord, Holy Father, almighty and eternal God, hear us and deign to send your holy angel to watch over everyone who comes to this place, and to protect, guard, defend and look after them': this prayer from the missal, which comes at the end of the Asperges on Sunday, before the parish mass, appears, with slight modifications, in different places in the Ritual: for example, for the blessing of a printery, house or school ('may the angels guard this school, with its teachers and pupils'). When a mother is blessed shortly before her child is born, the priest asks God to protect her from being waylaid by man's great enemy. The Ritual applies to the blessing of children the prayer from the feastday of the guardian angels (2 October): 'God our Father, in your loving providence you send your holy angels to watch over us. Hear our prayers, defend us always by their protection, and let us share your life with them for ever.' It also uses the prayer from the feast of St Michael to bless sick children: 'O God, in a wonderful way you direct the different ministries of men and angels: may those who serve you constantly in heaven keep the life of this child safe from all harm on earth.'

The 'miracles' of technology still leave room for help from the guardian angels: they keep us from all kinds of accidents. We can think of Apollo 13, which failed to reach the moon; or submarines which do not return to base; or the planes which crash or trains that get derailed despite all kinds of safety precautions. 'Lord, let your holy angels be in the carriages to defend from all dangers those who travel in them': the prayer for blessing railway carriages. In the blessing for a ship, the priest asks God to send his good angel from heaven, to protect the vessel and guard it and its passengers from all evil. 'Assign your angel to be companion to all who travel by air, to guard them and bring them safe and well to their destination', we read in the blessing for aeroplanes.

Like ignoring atomic energy
An exceptionally rich prayer, the anaphora of St Cyril of Alexandria, states that angels have an unlimited role as protectors: the protection they give extends to everything: 'Have mercy, O Lord, on your faithful here present; by the power of your Holy Cross and the protection of the angels, free us from all danger and all necessity: fire, flood, cold, robbers, serpents, wild animals, the attacks and snares of the devil, illnesses.'[6]

No. In the eyes of the Catholic Church, the reliable interpreter of Revelation, the guardian angels are not ethereal beings; they are not beings beyond our ken or mere symbols. They are real beings, powerful personalities, pure spirits who, when they come among us wearing visible shapes cause us to feel terror or wonder, as is evidenced by Holy Scripture.

This is attested by Blessed Peter Faber, one of the first disciples of St Ignatius Loyola: he was sent on a mission to Mainz but before setting up house, in a neighbourhood which had no great reputation, he first of all cast out the rebellious angels and established holy angels as invisible guardians. 'In each room of the house I said this prayer kneeling down: "We beseech you, Lord, to visit this dwelling; preserve it from all the snare of the enemy, so that your holy angels dwell here and guard us in peace, and that your blessing be upon us always, through Christ our Lord." I did this with true devotion and in the conviction that it was a right and proper way of acting on entering a place for the first time.

'Then, I proceeded to invoke the guardian angels of the neighbours and I felt that this, too, was a right and proper thing to do when one moves to a new neighbourhood. I prayed that my companions in this dwelling, and myself, might suffer no evil at the hands of the evil spirit in the locality, especially the spirit of fornication which must be found among the prostitutes, adulterers and licentious people who according to my information live there.'[7]

Is this the reaction of a timorous person, a visionary, a superstitious cleric? No. It is the attitude of a man of God whose lucid faith realises things—the snares of demons and the prayer of angels—which tend to escape people who have a more superficial view of life.

We do realize that the measures taken by Blessed Peter Faber in the sleezy quarter of Mainz are rather exceptional: not that they imply parting company with the genuine outlook and tradition of the Church but because they accord with them so perfectly that few Christians reach these standards—to their own cost.

As a German liturgist, Johannes Wagner, pointed out in a lecture on 'angels in the modern world', present-day coldness towards the invisible world is certainly not a sign of human progress. 'The fact that modern man, even the modern Christian, is no longer aware of or is not fully aware of the existence and power of angels, does not take away that existence or destroy that power. On the contrary, this ignorance impoverishes man's spirit, even to the extent of draining it of energy. It exposes him to grave dangers and deprives him of a powerful help.' The author uses this comparison to explain what he means: 'Atomic energy has existed since the beginning of the creation of the material world, long before man even suspected its existence. Similarly, the angels exist from the beginning of the creation of the spiritual world. And they will continue to exist, even if mankind ignores their existence for millions of years.'[8]

The modern world would gain nothing, and would lose a great deal, if it acted as if atomic energy were a myth or a crazy idea. Similarly, the Christian would gain nothing if he acted as if these invisible friendly presences, sent by God, were not following all his comings and goings, alert to help him and show him the way. If he acted like that he would be losing out at all levels of his life, in all the spheres in which he operates.[9]

Here below we will never know

Some readers must have been surprised to hear what Paul VI had to say about the role of angels in God's government of the world. They would have been surprised by the intimate relationship between Pius XI and his guardian angel and by Pius XII's inviting people to have a familiar relationship with their future companions in eternity: as also on seeing John XXIII, the Pope of Church renewal, expressing his desire that devotion to the guardian angels should increase among the faithful.

For this devotion to grow, we need to have a better knowledge of what angels are and what their role is. Yet it is difficult to get an exact idea of angels, and it is more difficult still to talk accurately about them. They are purely spiritual beings whom our eyes have never seen and whose existence we know about only through faith.

If it is difficult enough to write about the lives of the saints, who operate in thought and action at a level way above the ordinary, what chance have we of discussing non-material beings who overflow with intelligence, power and love?

This difficulty is underlined by one simple piece of information: although he had written a number of treatises on angels, St Thomas Aquinas confessed towards the end of his life that here on earth we cannot know exactly what angels are;[1] 'angelic substances are of a higher order than our minds; we cannot therefore apprehend them as they are in themselves.'[2]

St John Chrysostom was of the same mind. He explained to the Christians in Constantinople: 'The essence of our soul is something we cannot know exactly or, rather, we do not know at all. What is the substance of the soul? Is it air? Is it mind? Is it a breath? Is it a flame? Obviously, it is none of these because all these are corporeal whereas the soul is incorporeal.' We cannot know the essence of our soul: so how are we to know what angels are? 'No matter how much we explore the matter, we can never get to the bottom of it.'[3]

St Bernard, who wrote some magnificent pages on angels, recognizes his inability to deal with them in any sort of adequate way: 'What can I say about angelic spirits—I who am no more than a poor worm?'[4] All we can do is conjecture about their ministry, their hierarchy, using as a basis the names which Holy Scripture gives them.[5]

John Tauler, the fourteenth century German mystic, echoes these opinions in his sermon on the holy angels: 'I do not know in what terms we might and ought speak of these pure spirits, for they have neither hands nor feet nor face nor form nor matter; our spirit and mind cannot grasp a being who has none of these material properties: how, then, can we say what they are? We cannot know them, and that is not surprising, because we do not even know ourselves; we do not know the spirit which makes us human and through which we have received whatever good is in us; how can we then know these higher spirits whose nobility is so very much higher than anything to be found anywhere in the world?'[6]

Thoughts of astronauts

Difficulties of this sort do not go away: they have to do with the very nature of angels; but they are compounded by the crisis of faith at the present time. The Soviet astronaut Valentina Tereskova was reported as saying during a foreign tour: 'All the astronauts in the Soviet Union are Communists and atheists. None of us has seen out in space any angels or archangels, and I rather think that our American colleagues have had the same experience.' Interviewed about this statement, the American astronaut McDivit, who is a Christian, said: 'I don't see much difference between "down here" and "up there". If you live down here on friendly terms with the angels and with God, then you will live the same way up there. If you don't feel their presence on earth, you are not going to feel it on the Moon or on Mars.'[7]

Scientific progress has gone to many people's heads: they refuse to admit that anything exists unless they can see it through their research. This same attitude affects even believers. Nowadays, a Catholic who believes in realities whose existence is attested to only by faith, can even be regarded by his co-religionists as behind the times or naive—in the same way as if a teenager still believed babies are brought by the stork.

Paul VI often denounced the dangers of this 'technological spirit': 'Dominion over things and over natural forces, the pride of place given to what is practical and useful, a completely new lifestyle deriving from all kinds of applications of technology: all this suppresses in man his memory of God and drowns his need for faith and religion. Already Pius XII . . . in his 1953 radio message, spoke of this "technological spirit" which impregnates the modern approach.'

People see the maximum harnessing of the forces of nature as the supreme ideal of human life. The technological view of life has become a concrete form of materialism.[8]

To this 'technological spirit' we might add another difficulty, which is purely sociological in character—a widespread distaste for abstract reasoning. People nowadays acquire their knowledge mainly through their senses—we live in a civilization dominated by images—whereas faith requires a person to use his spirit, his mind and soul, for that is the only way to reach realities which are inaccessible to the senses. Thus, it has become more difficult, these days, to make the act of faith: at a purely sociological level it is more difficult to say, faithfully, 'I believe.'[9] Metaphysics is in crisis.

Paul VI also observed that the rush of modern life attracts people so much, impresses them so much, that they gorge themselves on images, thoughts, passions, desires, satisfactions, movement: they have no time left to listen to the word of Christ. And if they do hear something at school or in church, it all seems so complicated, so incoherent, so useless, that often they are more turned-off than turned-on, or go away with peculiar ideas rather than light to illuminate their souls and their lives.[10]

The spirit of 'questioning' everything has added to these difficulties. 'We are witnessing—everywhere—a phenomenon not so much of crude contradiction as of tendency to debate certain doctrinal truths: original sin; miracles, even Jesus' own miracles; the perpetual Virginity of Mary; even the Resurrection of Jesus Christ, which is the whole basis of faith. This more or less articulated "questioning" is a form of infidelity to the clear teaching of the Church.'[11] 'In a world of thought today everything is questioned; therefore, religion also is questioned,' Paul VI said. 'And it would appear that the spirit of modern man finds rest nowhere but in complete negation, in abandoning every certainty, every belief, as a person suffering from an eye illness finds no rest except in darkness.'[12]

Out of fashion
Is it surprising, then, that if they have to live in this sort of environment, Christians find it difficult to believe in the existence

36

of guardian angels? Is it surprising that, in a world drunk with technological progress, there seems to be no room for the activity of angels? And is it surprising if some writers suffering from desacralization reduce to myths or symbols the interventions of angels recorded in sacred scripture?

Between the two extremes—of full acceptance of the traditional theology of angels, and total denial of it—there is a middle ground, half yes, half no, a grey, rather than black or white. Given that there are feast-days of angels in the liturgical calendar, and that they are mentioned in prefaces and the Our Father alludes to them as models of obedience to the will of God, and that every night the prayer of Compline expressly invokes the protection of the guardian angels: given all this, people will not deny them their mission or role; but they will say these prayers in a mindless, heartless sort of way like a record-player playing a record: a sort of imitation of that neurotic lady who got nervous every time she thought of death, yet said the three parts of the Rosary every day. 'But, my dear', a friend said to her, 'why are you so afraid of death, you who love our Lady and ask her one hundred and fifty times a day for the grace of a happy death?' 'Me, pray for the grace of a happy death? Never! I get a fright every time I hear the word death!' 'Still you say in every Hail Mary: "Pray for us, sinners, now and at the hour of our death." Every Rosary has one hundred and fifty Hail Marys. Count them yourself . . .' How many clerics are there who, ever sceptical when lay people talk to them about angels, invoke every night at Compline the help of the guardian angels, perhaps without realizing it . . .

Caricatures of angels
There is, additionally, one other culprit behind the decline of belief in angels—a certain type of adulterated religious art which completely misrepresents angels.

It is perfectly understandable how certain representations of angels can turn people off devotion to them.[13] Fleshy or dainty angels are a disgusting caricature, just as ridiculous plaster statues of our Lady do nothing for the Mother of God.[14] What a distance there is between these affected angels and the way angels appear in the Book of Daniel or Revelation: there they are frightening, shocking—causing the prophet and the evangelist to prostrate themselves on the ground.[15] St John receives such a shock that he thinks he is in the presence of the Almighty. The angel invites him to get up and to keep adoration for God alone (Rev 19:10).

'If it is true that art is not necessary for saints' piety, still it is necessary for ours, for the piety of the faithful people of whom we form part', wrote Cardinal Journet. 'I know people who are helped to pray by the harmony of Chartres Cathedral. I also know that those terribly artificial representations of St Joseph, St Louis Gonzaga, St Francis de Sales . . . which they were exposed to when they were children, have given them an indelible false picture of those saints, who were in fact fine, vigorous people.'[16]

At the Council of Fermo (1726) the Church found it necessary to strike a note of warning against the lascivious beauty of certain works of art depicting angels; yet we have already seen how the angels of the gothic cathedrals and the angels of Fra Angelico encourage one to pray. 'Devotion to the angels is inevitably nourished through contact with these works of art. Just by contemplating them we feel purer, we feel urged to see God and love him.'[17]

However, it must be recognized that it is not at all easy for a painter or sculptor to depict angels. Obviously they need technical and artistic ability and good religious knowledge: but perhaps they also need to have a certain personal familiarity with these spiritual beings.

I met in Rome at one time a painter, who exercised her art as an apostolate in former East Germany. Before beginning to paint she spent a while in prayer before the Blessed Sacrament—and this helps her paintings lead one to pray. She received many Church commissions. This lady could easily have established herself in Austria or what was West Germany: she could have done well. But she preferred to work in the shadows of the Church of Silence, convinced—quite rightly—that sacred art is a very valuable way of offering spiritual resistance to atheistic materialism.

Chemistry, a substitute for prayer?
The apparent uselessness of angels is another factor which gets in the way of belief in them. Modern man believes that he can get from the resources of nature what his ancestors used look to God for. 'In former times,' a with-it preacher argued, 'peasants used to have processions to pray for good harvests. But they have progressed: now they use fertilizers.' Chemistry is proving to be far better than prayer.

The same sort of argument is used in connection with angels. Social security, health insurance, accident insurance, the police system, advances in medicine, etc: all this seems to give modern man adequate protection against the hazards of life. Therefore, there is no room any longer for God and his angels; they have no role to play in the difficulties of daily life.

As if God had not warned man that he laboured in vain unless God watched over him (cf. Ps 127). Is it fertilizer that really protects the land from hail and frost, flood and drought? Whether we like it or not, in the last analysis, 'good things and bad, life and death, poverty and wealth, come from the Lord' (Sir 11:14).

If we went too far in one direction in the past that is no reason why we should go too far in the other now. Maybe some Christians did give too much importance to angels in the past: but nowadays they are very generally neglected. Whatever new discoveries science has made, St Thomas' principle still holds: in all his physical interventions in the universe, God makes use of the ministry of angels.[18] They are, as it were, God's arms and hands.

'Ministry': this word also contains the key to another problem—that of thinking that angels are in competition with God. If we regarded angels as *interfering*, this would lead to eliminating angels on the grounds that they clutter up the scene and cause a nuisance.

An example? Pope John XXIII liked to attribute to inspiration by his guardian angel the good ideas he got in the course of the day. We might ask: is that not pious exaggeration or just a figure of speech, for, in the Mass for peace, there is a prayer which says that it is God himself who gives us 'our good desires, our wise counsels and good works'? In other words: either these inspirations come from God or they come from one's guardian angel. But why could they not come from both, by different titles? Why not see God as their source and the angel as the channel they come through? There is no opposition or interference involved between source and channel: it is, rather, a matter of continuity and cooperation. Recognizing the secondary role of the channel does not deny the primary role of the source.

No need to go into the stratosphere
If one has a distorted view of God, seeing him more as a judge than as a father, this could also affect one's faith in the angels' role as guardians. How could anyone imagine a terrifying God lovingly entrusting every man and woman to an angel, to be with him in all his or her comings and goings? To understand this gesture of

a God who is love, 'in a corrupt world where everything has its price' (Pius XII) and to avoid measuring God's attributes by the standard of human virtues, we need to rise above popular notions. It is not an easy thing to do, and few people do it. A person needs special, supernatural help to succeed at it. As St Teresa of Lisieux observed, 'few indeed are those souls who do not measure God's goodness according to their own limited ideas'.

Thus, left to himself, a person will not admit that God entrusted the guardianship of a single human being to one of these beings overflowing with intelligence, strength and beauty. Only a soul enlightened by a living faith can acknowledge this prodigy of love which captivated St Bernard. 'It is a wonderful effect of his goodness and one of the greatest earnests of his love that we can receive.' God orders his angels, 'those spirits, so high, so happy, so close to him, so united to him, so submissive to him, his true friends and familiars: for our sakes he orders them to come down on earth'.[19] Why should we be surprised if God allocates angels to serve men, the Abbot of Clairvaux asks, when he has in fact sent them his very own Son? 'The very king of angels came not to be served but to serve, and to give his life as a ransom for many.' By showing us God's immeasurable goodness, the dogma of the Incarnation and of the Redemption sheds a stronger light on Church teaching on the guardian angels.

The more we use ideas from a secularized world as tests of religious truth, the more doubtful the existence of guardian angels will seem to us. Whereas, the more we take God's word as our rule, as interpreted by the Catholic Church, the quicker will we solve any difficulties which arise. A strong faith will clear up difficulties, just as wind dispels fog. As Blessed Josemaría Escrivá put it, 'You say that in such surroundings there are many occasions of going astray? That's true, but is there not also the presence of the guardian angels? ...'[20]

In addition to showing us God's incomprehensible love for men, faith also shows us his infinite wisdom and power, which are reflected in the world of the angels. We could say, applying to the existence of angels St Thomas' words in praise of the Real Presence in the hymn *Lauda Sion*:

> And if senses fail to see,   *Et si sensus deficit*
> Faith alone the truth awaketh *Ad firmandum cor sincerum*
> To behold the mystery.   *Sola fides suficit.*

Faith alone suffices, whereas all the other reasons are in themselves insufficient for establishing beyond all doubt that angels exist. This means that a Christian believes in angels not because it *makes sense* that there are spiritual beings, created pure spirits, between God, who is uncreated spirit, and man, made up of body and soul. Nor does he believe in them because in certain ancient and contemporary non-Christian religions we can find certain parallels to good and bad angels, possibly survivals from a primitive revelation. We believe because the Church, the faithful interpreter of Revelation, presents their existence and activity as a truth revealed by God himself. 'Only through faith do we know the existence of angels', states St Augustine.[21]

If we want to set about finding angels there is no need to go into the stratosphere. To hear them and find them all we need do is move on to the supernatural level: there, as the same saint puts it, we can see them through 'the eyes of faith'.

Over-sensitivity towards modern susceptibilities could make a Christian turn his back on the light God is offering him in Revelation: this would leave him in the darkness of ignorance and error and could even mean offence to God through refusing to accept his word.[22] It is blasphemy to question God's truthfulness.[23]

This tendency to conform to a secularized world can lead people to abdicate in all sorts of pathetic ways. To win the approval of people of little faith, some Catholics do not mind displeasing God. They forget what St Paul says: 'If I were still pleasing men, I should not be a servant of Christ' (Gal 1:10). What they seem to be saying is: 'If I were to accept all the various teachings of the Church, then I would cease to be acceptable to people.'

In pursuit of angels

Another, final, series of difficulties can arise out of Holy Scripture itself, when it speaks of the activity of angels. Paul VI pointed out that 'difficulties of faith can also derive from philosophical, exegetical and historical studies of this first source of revealed truth —Holy Scripture. Deprived of its complement of Tradition and the authoritative help given by the Magisterium of the Church, even the very study of the Bible is full of doubts and problems which disconcert rather than reinforce faith.'[24]

Let us look at a few passages of Scripture which could disconcert the uninitiated. The Book of Daniel shows us angels in conflict among themselves (10:13). We believe that the angels enjoy an undisturbed happiness; whereas Isaiah (33:7) says that the angels of peace will weep. The Second Book of Kings (19:35) credits an exterminating angel with the death of 185,000 Assyrian soldiers in one night; whereas the exegetes, following the Greek historian Herodotus, attribute the deaths to an epidemic of plague spread by rats. Was it God himself or was it an angel who appeared to Moses in the burning bush? Does the expression 'angel of the Lord' (or angel of Yahweh) refer to God or to an angel?

Tradition helps sort out difficulties of this kind. As St Thomas Aquinas explains it, the expressions used by Daniel and Isaiah are not to be taken literally: they are a translation of spiritual facts into metaphors drawn from human experience.[25]

An invasion of rats into the Assyrian camp does not exclude the intervention of an exterminating angel. Why could the angel *not* have used an army of rats to spread plague? Dominion of animals by a pure spirit is in the order of things. It should not surprise us any more than a shepherd's control over his flock would: the shepherd acts on the sheep's external senses (hearing, touch, etc); the angel acts on their internal senses (imagination, memory) to control their external behaviour.[26]

As regards the references now to God (or Yahweh), now to his angel, St Thomas solves the problem by making a distinction.[27] When angels intervene it is always on God's orders; therefore the sacred writer attributes this intervention now to God, now to the angel who is an instrumental cause, i.e. he is the instrument or device through which God acts: 'just as the pope is said to absolve someone even if the rite of absolution be given by someone else.'[28]

Besides, this alternation of complementary expressions is often found in ordinary life. When the Cardinal Secretary of State, for example, addresses a letter to a Social Week on behalf of the pope, the newspapers refer to the *Pope's letter*, the *Cardinal's letter*: it does not matter. There is a moral unity just as—on another plane and in another manner—God and the angel he sends to men form a moral unity. The moral unity does not involve physical identity between the one who issues and the one who carries out the order: they are two distinct beings.[29]

The demythologizing movement leads certain interpreters to systematically exclude angels from the Bible: they do this by interpreting some mentions of an angel as being really references to God, and others as referring really to natural phenomena.

Mistakes of this kind (which cause confusion to believers)

would be avoided if, in addition to using profane sciences these experts were to use Tradition and the Magisterium to shed light on the Bible, according to the norm Paul VI reminded them of; it would also help if we adapted ourselves less to the outlook of a secularized world and did not give so much credence to slogans as superficial as they are aggressive—slogans, such as: 'People nowadays will never accept that! No one believes that any more! Have you taken a poll? How are you so sure?'

Unless a lay person looks to Tradition and the Magisterium, he or she will never find satisfactory answers to the questions Bible-reading raises. Instead of giving him light and certainty about angels, the Bible could lead in the direction of problems and doubts.

Unless Holy Scripture is read with the aid of the light thrown on it by the Church, then, in league with a debased religious art, the worship of technology, the phenomenon of secularization and that critical spirit which puts question marks beside everything, people's faith in the existence of angels *whom God associates in his government of the world*[30] can be corroded.

Cracks and ambushes

No Catholic with clear ideas in his head would deny that angels exist; but that angels play a necessary role, in the economy of salvation, by guarding human beings (including twentieth century human beings, revelling in the conquests of science): this is something which many Christians would regard as somewhat debatable.

Modern man, like his predecessors, needs the protection of angels for two essential reasons, neither of which has anything to do with the evolution of society or with technological progress: first, because he is and will continue to be a defective creature; second, because he is the target of continuous attack and ambush by Satan.

The argument that man is morally self-sufficient is not a new one; it is perennial. St Thomas Aquinas was quite familiar with it. He refers to it in the first line of the first page of the treatise on angels in the *Summa Theologiae*.

Guardians are assigned, he says, to those who cannot or do not know how to protect themselves: children and the sick have guardians. But men can guard themselves through the use of their free will and their ordinary knowledge of the natural law. Therefore angels serve no purpose.

How does the Common Doctor of the Church answer this objection? St Thomas admits that men are aware of the natural law and do have free will. But he adds—and this is the core of his argument—this awareness and this free will are insufficient. They are real, to be sure, but they are insufficient.

Thanks to free will, 'men can avoid evil to some degree but not completely, for their affection for the Good is weakened by the passions of the soul. Similarly, universal knowledge of the natural law, which is a natural endowment of man, directs men to what is good, but not completely, for when they try to apply the universal principles of natural law to particular acts they very often fall down.' Thus, Scripture can say that 'The thoughts of mortal men are fearful and our plans uncertain.' From this it follows that 'it is necessary for men to be guarded by angels.'[1]

Christian revelation shows us that this disequilibrium which affects man's faculties and deflects his behaviour is a result of original sin. That sin has had a traumatic effect on human faculties: man's reason is blunted, especially with regard to moral decision; his will becomes hardened against the true good; sustained virtuous activity becomes increasingly difficult, and his concupiscence grows in ardour.[2]

This substratum of evil, a commentator on St Thomas writes, is the reason why man no longer has a natural taste for God but, rather, finds it a struggle to submit to God and raise his heart up to God; it is the reason for his strange facility for turning his back on God, for doing without God . . .[3] 'We are inclined by nature to follow what is worse rather than what is better,' writes St Teresa in her *Life* (Chapter II).

Blessed Josemaría Escrivá's recommendation is that we 'must learn to speak to the angels. Turn to them now. . . . Ask them to bring up to the Lord your good will, which, by the grace of God, has grown out of your wretchedness like a lily grown on a dunghill. Holy angels, our guardians: "Defend us in battle, so that we do not perish at the final judgment."'[4]

The damage done by original sin is aggravated by people's personal sins, by their vices and, sometimes, by their inherited tendencies.

It is to protect us, debilitated as we are in our minds and wills, that God sends his angels. 'All those men and women whom you behold', Bossuet, the great seventeenth century French preacher says, addressing the angels, 'are sick and wretched people, whose extreme need cries out for your help!' Developing his thought, he goes on: 'All men are prisoners, weighed down by the chains of this mortal body; you free spirits, help them to carry this oppressive weight; keep up the soul which ought to tend towards heaven, do not let it be drawn down to earth by the weight of the flesh. All men are ignorant because they walk in the midst of darkness: spirits who see the pure light, dispel the clouds which envelope us. All men are attracted by what appeals to their senses: you who drink at the very fountain of chaste and intellectual pleasures, soothe our thirst with drops of the heavenly dew. All men have in the depth of their souls an unhappy seed of envy, which continuously produces argument, rancour, gossip, defamation, division: contemplative spirits, peaceful spirits, calm the storm of our angers; sweeten the bitterness of our hatreds; be invisible mediators who will reconcile in our Lord our ulcerous hearts.'[5]

A curious thing, which reveals the traces of original sin in man's way of reasoning: in a false sense of self-sufficiency, the modern world raises itself up against the teaching of the Church on 'man's propensity to be unbalanced and evil'; yet, at the same time, and in literature, it accepts the most desolate descriptions of human corruption. A case of double standards! Pessimistic views of man's corrupt nature are accepted if they come from philosophers and writers, but rejected if they come from the Church. Yet Catholic theology is infinitely less depressing than the approach to be found in existentialist writers: the Church states that original sin has weakened man's tendency towards the Good—but has not vitiated the very structure of his nature: man is not fundamentally bad. Far from leading us towards barren pessimism and despair, the Church shows us the lights and energies God is offering us: she opens up horizons of salvation and happiness.

There is another curious fact which reveals the lack of balance resulting from original sin and the way Christians are contaminated by the spirit of the world: they frequently side-step the dogma of original sin. This is a truth revealed by God, 'which we no longer dare to face', was how Cardinal Garrone put it. 'Does anyone preach about original sin any more?'[6] The same question might be also asked of certain catechisms.

If original sin and its unfortunate effects on man's intellectual stability and moral health are denied, in theory and in practice, this means implicitly denying the need for any kind of protection by angels: in the same way as someone who enjoys good health has no need of a doctor or a well-balanced person has no particular need of advice.

But if we accept the Catholic doctrine of original sin, this means that we admit the need for some remedy to it. And the Church gives us that remedy in the form of protection by angels.

The effects of original sin are not felt only in exceptional situations. Original sin leaves its mark on our very make-up; its effects are permanent, like the effects of chronic illness or some congenital disability. A shortsighted person is shortsighted day and night, in town and on the beach, in the factory and in the cinema. Similarly, man's moral conscience and will are defective, in some way or another, all the time. This permanent disability is in continuous need of that therapy which comes in the form of grace and of guardianship by angels.

Hardly daring to mention the devil

There is another reason why we are in constant need of being helped by that spiritual being whom God has commissioned to be our protector—the attacks which we continually suffer from that other spiritual being, the devil.

The devil? 'Nowadays, hardly anyone dares to speak of the devil', Cardinal Garrone wrote. 'A kind of conspiracy of silence prevails on this subject. And when the silence is broken, it is by individuals who assume a knowing look or with surprising temerity question the very existence of the devil. This certitude is based on a constant teaching whose source lies in the Gospel and the Old Testament. It would be foolhardy to reject it. The existence, the nature, and the action of the devil are profoundly mysterious. The only wise attitude for us to take on this question is to accept the affirmations of our Faith without seeking to know more than Revelation has deemed prudent to tell us.'[7]

Lending assent to statements of the faith—one of things the Church used to propose every day (up to the recent reform of the Breviary) to priests and to lay people who read the Divine Office was a passage from the first letter of St Peter (5:8), which occurred at the start of Compline: 'Brethren, be sober, be watchful. Your adversary the devil prowls around like a roaring lion, seeking someone to devour. Resist him, firm in the faith.' St Bernard links this passage with a verse from the Book of Job, where Satan says, 'I have been to and fro on the earth, and walking up and down on it' (1:7) and emphasizes the perseverance and obstinacy of the devil.[8]

Compline concludes with another reference to the devil, which is accompanied with an invocation to the guardian angels: 'Visit this house, Lord, we beseech you, and thrust far from it the devil and his temptations: may your angels make their home here to guard us in peace, and let your blessing be on us always.' It is no more an accident that angels and devils are mentioned here in the same breath than, for example, if a good man and an evil man happened to be on the same bus. The fact is part of God's providential design: in order to counteract the devil's actions on men, God has entrusted men to the protection of angels.

In other words, there is a certain control operating. God could have thrown the rebellious angels into hell once and for all, immediately after they sinned—as he will do at the end of time.[9] He preferred to leave them a certain freedom of action, in order to use them in his service: he uses the devil's power and malice to test our virtue. There is nothing in the universe that God has not included in his plans. In one way or another, every single thing is at God's service; nothing is outside his control.[10] God uses the malice of the devils to achieve something good for us—to help us exercise virtue.[11]

A providential role

Obviously, many people would live mediocre lives or slide steadily into evil if Providence did not put them in a position which obliged them to opt for good or for evil. Without these tests, would Job have ever attained heroic virtue? The angels are to be seen as executives of God's designs who point the elect in the way of spiritual progress.

The good angels help us to progress; they raise us up towards goodness and keep us away from evil; the bad angels also contribute to our progress—indirectly—by encouraging us to do evil and by giving us thereby an opportunity to react in the other direction.[12] The devils are actors in the history of salvation: they have a providential role here below, putting men to the test by way of temptation.[13]

Nor are the devil's evil powers completely free-roving; they are subject to control; God holds them in check. Like the waves of the sea evoked in the Book of Job (38:11), before letting them tempt men God has told the devils: 'Thus far shall you come, and no farther, and here shall your proud waves be stayed.'

St Augustine makes the following observation: 'The devil would often wish to do harm but his power is subordinated to another power. If the devil could do as much harm as he wished, there would be no just people in the world.'[14]

It is difficult for us to imagine the power of devils. Always within the limits laid down by Providence, and respecting the natural order, they have power over the world of matter.[15] They can play with material things the same way a child plays with marbles. Although man's mind and will are forbidden territory to them, they still have access to his external senses and lower faculties—imagination, sensibility, memory. By influencing these faculties they indirectly reach his mind and will. Just think of the role sense-images, feelings and impulses play in a person's behaviour and it is easy to realize that the devil has a great deal of scope for influencing our decisions and behaviour. He can awaken sense-images and cause us to have feelings which affect our thinking and incline our will in the direction that suits him.

Given that they are intellectually superior to men, 'demons are much more capable than all our psychiatrists and psychologists; they are much more experienced than all our moralists and all our politicians.'[16] 'Their natural power is really amazing', a spiritual writer observes. 'They can excite us, stir up the images dormant in our imagination causing the more dangerous ones to grow, because they know that these are the ones you prefer . . . They slide like serpents, they jump like lions. They can attach themselves to you like your own shadow; they harass you; they lay siege to you.'[17]

Satan wears disguise
C.S. Lewis describes the devil's tactics in great detail in his book *The Screwtape Letters*. St Paul sums them up in a single phrase: 'Satan disguises himself as an angel of light' (2 Cor 11:14). A modern exegete asks whether the Apostle is referring here to an apocryphal life of Adam, where Satan appears to Eve in the form of an angel of light when he tempts her for the second time. Possibly. The Apostle's main purpose is to make us realize that the Evil One has the ability to assume the appearance of goodness.[18]

When devils try to mislead us, they deck themselves with aspects of truth in order to make themselves acceptable. When they propose sin, they give it an appearance of virtue. Man is deceived and yields to the temptation. 'Thus the intellect falls into error, misled by apparent truth, just as the will is inclined towards evil by apparent good.'[19]

Devils do not work on an abstract and general level: their tactic is always tailored to the particular situation. They approach their victim on his weak flank, or through something he is particularly interested in. And with consummate ability they advance gradually, taking no short-cuts. Usually, Satan does not have recourse to exceptional methods—such as obsession, possession or apparitions, the sort we find in the lives of some saints. He is content with using the ordinary tools of his trade, working dexterously on our imagination. He manipulates images with truly diabolic art.

A contemporary theolgian, C.D. Boulogne, writes: 'The wisdom of the greatest human genius is no match for the devil's prodigious skill. The soul's fortress has all sorts of cracks through which evil can insinuate itself! The first thing the devil works on is the imagination and he creates a certain restlessness through sense-images which coax one's self-love. He finds a powerful ally in the tendency we all have to day-dream—dreams which too often absorb our attention and take us away from reality. By means of sense-images the devil obtains access to our reason and clouds our judgment, because up to this point he dresses things in mystery and enchantment. In this way he seeks to provoke that cowardly and perverted curiosity which causes us to loiter in that *chiaroscuro*, in that shadowy area where colours and shapes fade to the point where we can no longer make them out and no longer think of exercising our judgment . . . Tranquillized in this way, our conscience falls asleep.'[20]

Chapters 40 and 41 of the Book of Job show us two monsters, Behemoth and Leviathan, who are stronger than all other animals rolled into one. With other Doctors of the Church, St Thomas Aquinas sees in this physcial superiority an image of Satan's pre-eminence over man: man, with only his natural lights to guide him, is incapable of discovering and freeing himself from the devices Satan uses to induce him to sin.[21] Anyone who thinks he can be up to Satan looks as silly as a bulldog trying to take on a rhinoceros.

Tauler, the fourteenth century German mystic, describes in this way the manoeuvres devils use to undermine fervent souls: they use, he says, all their astuteness. The malice they apply is indescribable: a man would have to be continually on guard and heavily protected to keep this enemy at bay. They are very good at dissimulation and often use things which have an appearance of goodness. They almost always try to get a person to be overactive and, if they fail to do this, they induce him to act in a way which seems good, and then they insinuate the idea that he is doing well, that he should be satisfied with himself and that he should not complicate his life. This is a very disconcerting temptation, because as St Bernard says 'on the way to God stopping means going backwards'. This is the state where we find all the unworldy souls who say, 'I do as many good words as So-and-So or So-and So; that is more than enough because I have no reason to aim higher than they; I will keep to what I am doing.'[22] Overactivity, spreading oneself too thinly, self-satisfaction, together with carelessness about spiritual progress—this is what the devil is aiming at in his tactics with priests, religious and fervent Christians.

Monsieur Vincent puts us on our guard . . .
In the same sort of way, St Vincent de Paul points out to the Sisters
of Charity the subtle way the devil attacks one of the weapons of
spiritual life—prayer, especially morning prayer which infuses
faith and love into all the profane activities of the day ahead: 'The
devil does everything he can to prevent us from praying, because
he knows well that if the spirit of frivolous thoughts is the first to
fill us, it will be in control the whole day long.'[23]

There we have St Vincent, famous for his active apostolate:
what he says echoes St John of the Cross, the soaring contemplative: in the *Living Flame of Love* and *Spiritual Canticle* the saint
describes the ends to which devils go to draw our souls away from
contemplation. His perseverance really is impressive; a commentator on St John of the Cross writes: 'It is remarkable to see the
regard Satan has for contemplation, the importance he gives it.
Satan thinks that he gains more by even slightly damaging the
prayer of a contemplative than by doing a lot of damage to a whole
crowd of people who are less advanced spiritually. He even sees
this as a greater advantage than getting many souls to commit
grave sins, for these souls have little or nothing to lose, whereas
the contemplative soul has a valuable capital—just as it is much
more serious to lose a small amount of gold than a large quantity
of base metal.'[24]

Similarly, a reader of the Gospel is amazed when he comes to
those passages where our Lord meets up with diabolical forces.
'When Jesus appears among men, at his every step we hear un-
clean spirits shouting in the bodies and souls of the possessed, the
reason being that the devils know that the Holy One of God, who
is going to crush them, has entered the scene.'[25] 'If the passage in
Luke 4:6 is taken seriously—as also many of Jesus' actual words,
not forgetting what St Paul and St John have to say—we will be
led to believe that the devil's power over the world (*Daemon-
isierung der Welt*) is much more extensive and much more profound than is commonly supposed.'[26]

One fact which is quite revealing in this connection is pointed
out by L. Bouyer: 'When it [the Church] wants to bless any living
being or element, it invariably begins by showing that it considers
this creature to have been in the power of the devil until that
moment and believes it must first of all recapture it from the devil
and drive him out.

'When the Church consecrates a temple of worship so as to

establish itself within it, it exorcizes its entire site. When it blesses water, oil, or any other raw material taken from the world for its own use, or when it wants to incorporate into itself through holy Baptism a person born in this world, the same ceremony precedes every positive act of consecration.

'In so doing, the Church indicates that its work of perpetuating Christ on earth, of fulfilling Christ, is fundamentally a reconquest, a transfer of property acquired by force, an expulsion. It is a question of recapturing, element by element, person by person, this world where the devil and his cohorts have been able— through man's sins, through his idolatry—to arrogate a quasi-divine sovereignty, and of eradicating these evil spirits from the earth. The Church's procedure, therefore, is to advance like an army in battle array . . .'[27]

Two invisible blocs

Revelation, therefore, shows us that the devil has extensive powers over the world and over each individual: we really cannot grasp the scale of his influence, ignorant as we are of everything to do with these incorporeal beings. Man could never have had any sure knowledge of the devil's powers, if God had not revealed this mystery to him. At the present time when there seems to be a kind of conspiracy of silence, even among Christians, about these powers, there is all the more need for them to be spoken about openly.

Spiritual writers have in fact pointed out that one of the devil's blatant victories consists in getting people to let down their guard by forgetting about him and his influence.

By being practically unknown to and ignored by a large number of Christians, Satan is able to act with much more freedom. He is an implacable enemy whose constant presence at our side we too often forget. He is like a kind of fifth columnist whose strength and activities are known only to a very few.

The protective presence of angels at our side is called for by this insidious presence of devils—in addition to that other factor, the wound caused by original sin. Every man, every woman, every child, every adolescent, is continuously being looked after by his or her guardian angel—just as he is also the constant object of the devil's scheming.

If we transfer from the personal to the social level this information our faith gives us or look at it in a global context we will be able to understand certain things—at first sight surprising—which we find in the Fathers of the Church or in the masters of the Spiritual life. These men and women were being realists not visionaries when, like St Ambrose, they said that 'earth and heaven are teeming with angels and devils'.

Just as during the world wars the west was divided into two military groupings, so too there are two invisible forces battling it out in the world—the good angels and the unfaithful angels. The Apocalypse gives us an insight into the scope and vehemence of this gigantic conflict, as does the mysterious passage in St Paul where he exhorts the faithful to fight with the weapons of faith against the spiritual forces of evil spread throughout the heavens and against the princes of this world of darkness (cf. Eph 6:11-12); and also the prayer to St Michael the Archangel, prince of the heavenly host, which used to be included in the prayers at the end of low Mass.

In the lives of the Fathers it is told how one day St Isidore the hermit went up on to the roof of his hut in the company of Abbot Moses whom the devil of impurity had been tempting for some time. 'Look towards the west', Isidore told his visitor. The abbot saw a noisy host of devils as if preparing for battle. Then the hermit said, 'Look east', and Abbot Moses saw a countless multitude of holy angels—the heavenly host, more resplendent than the sun. 'Those whom you saw in the west', said the hermit, 'are those who attack the saints; those you have seen in the east are those whom God has sent to succour the saints. You must see that we have numbers and strength on our side.' The holy Abbot Moses returned to his cell comforted.[28]

Speaking to the faithful about the heavenly armies, St John Chrysostom also reminds them about devils, those barbarous and ferocious beings who fill the air around us, ready to do battle. Fortunately God has opposed them with armies of good angels. The Bishop of Constantinople compares these angels to the troops garrisoned in cities on the frontiers of the empire to defend it from barbarian incursions.[29]

'There are more on our side'

St Thomas Aquinas has summed up this doctrine very succinctly in an article in his *Summa Theologiae* where he discusses the forces the devils employ against men.[30] A friend of dialogue, he first puts an objection: it is not a fair fight if the weak are set against the strong and the ignorant against the clever. Now, men are weak and ignorant, whereas devils are strong and clever. Therefore, God, who is the author of all justice, would not permit men to be attacked by devils.

Here is the way he replies to the objection: 'So that the contest should not be an unequal one, men get some compensation, first through the help of God's grace, and second, through the guardianship of the angels. Thus, Elisha said to his servant, "Do not be afraid, for there are more on our side than on theirs".'[31]

Commenting on this reply, a contemporary theologian emphasizes the importance St Thomas gives to the protection afforded by the angels, comparing it to the role of divine grace in the economy of salvation.[32]

The final verse of the hymn *Aeterne rector siderum*, which the Church sings on the feast of the guardian angels, links up these two things in a similar way: 'Glory be to God the Father, who by means of his angels guards those whom his Son has ransomed and whom the Holy Spirit has sanctified.'

No. The guardian angel is not a part of the decor in the scenario where men live out their lives and where their eternal destiny is decided. He has an important role. Has he not been destined by God to the service of man, as the Letter to the Hebrews says?

The history of nations and of their leading figures is studied and written about. This history deals with visible facts and analyses those affairs where they can exert some control. To complete the picture it would be necessary also to write a history of the invisible facts and events they do not control, a fabric woven out of the influence exerted by both the holy angels and the devils—on chiefs of state, on politicians, on thinkers, educators and artists, on people who work in the media, on business life, on the world of fashion, etc.

This complementary information would explain many things which we can only partly explain.

The prince of lies

For example, can we even suspect to what extent diabolical powers influenced the ideology of a Hitler or a Stalin?

In a study of the action of Satan in our time, Dom Alois Mager, Dean of the Faculty of Theology at Salzburg, refers to the influence of demoniacal powers on Adolf Hitler and on national socialism.[33]

'He [the devil] was a murderer from the beginning, and has nothing to do with the truth, because there is no truth in him.'[34]

From these words of Jesus, Dom Mager concludes that there are two key signs of the devils' world—falsehood and murder. He finds both these signs in the *Fuehrer* and his *Weltanschauung*: 'In calling national socialism the *mendacium incarnatum*, falsehood incarnate, Pius XI could not have described it more exactly. Falsehood annihilates spiritual life; murder annihilates the life of the body. Annihilation—that is the tactic of the forces of Satan. It is significant that there is no word that occurs more often in the speeches of Hitler and his Nazi leaders, and in the Nazi press, than the words destruction, elimination, annihilation.

'There is no more compact, more precise, more appropriate definition of Hitler than that of (. . .) *medium of Satan* (. . .). During the Nuremburg trials, General Jodl said of him that he was a great man, but an infernal great man.' Monsignor J.B. Neuhausler, who was a prisoner in a Nazi concentration camp, and later auxiliary bishop of Munich, sums up the essence of Nazism in these words: 'Satan and national socialism are linked to one another.'

A French philosopher, Jean Guitton, arrives at the same conclusion: 'Can anything match the Hitler phenomenon? In the space of twelve years, a man who was neither a strategist nor a remarkable politician, a man who only had the frenetic strength of a *medium*, was able, on his own, to hallucinate an entire people: in previous revolutions it needed a whole set of geniuses to do that sort of thing. Hitler did on his own what it took Rousseau, Mirabeau, Robespierre, Bonaparte to do together. And he was on the point of pulling it off. One cannot avoid getting the impression that, in this unique case, which we have witnessed, to produce as extraordinary a phenomenon as this, there occurred something analogous to what demonologists call enchantment, possession, that is to say, a take-over of a human personality by another infrahuman and superhuman personality.'[35]

He has always been a deceiver
Turning to atheistic communism, we might ask whether Catholics are aware that Pius XI also connects communism's origins with the influence of the devil.

The first page of his encyclical *Divini Redemptoris* (on atheistic communism) recalls the promise of a divine Redeemer, hope in whom softened man's regrets for 'the paradise of pleasure' and sustained him on his journey through history. In the fullness of time the Saviour came, far exceeding man's hopes, and inaugurated a new civilization. 'But ever since Adam's unhappy fall, and in bitter consequence of that hereditary sin, virtue has had a bitter struggle to wage against the suggestions of vice, and the wily old tempter has never desisted from misleading men by false promises. The result has been one unheaval after another through the course of ages, until we have come to the revolution of our own time, now either raging or else frowning its menace in nearly every part of the world, exceeding in violence and magnitude any persecution which the Church has ever sustained . . . (This peril) is none other than bolshevist communism, atheistic communism': Pius XI refers to 'the result', the intimate connection between Satan's constant machinations and the advent of atheistic communism. Pius XI connects Satan with the origins of communism, without denying that other factors were also responsible—factors such as a decline in faith, economic liberalism, social injustice crying to heaven.

However, the influence of the fallen angels on cultural, financial, political and military aspects of the lives of peoples should not cause us to forget that the angels of light also exercise a real influence on the world.

The hymn *Aeterne rector siderum* referred to above also recalls the different ways these spirits intervene in the lives of nations as regards security, public health and social peace. One of the most fine souls of the twentieth century, Cardinal Faulhaber, Archbishop of Munich, once gave a sermon in which he described the role of the guardian angels of nations, using Scripture as his basis.[36]

The epic story of St Joan of Arc is a splendid illustration of the intervention of St Michael and the angels in the affairs of an earthly kingdom. What is exceptional in this case is not that they take an interest in temporal affairs but that they play a visible, audible role—whereas normally their action is hidden.

Only God knows fully the scope and depth of the influence of angels and devils in the shaping of human history. On the day of the Final Judgment the world will be astounded when it discovers it. At that moment everything which today is naturally hidden to the eyes of our body will come to light: *Quidquid latet apparebit.*

To guard you in all your ways

Some years ago there was a style in religious 'art' which liked to show the guardian angel looking after little boys or girls in dangerous situations. The trouble with that sort of thing is that it gives the impression that angels have nothing to do with adults: babies and children need their protection, but surely teenagers and adults can look after themselves . . .

That kind of approach is quite mistaken, Romano Guardini pointed out.[1] In fact, teenagers and adults need the protection of angels more than children do. Men and women meet difficulties and temptations which children never experience; therefore, the help they get should fit the need. This is shown, as we have seen, by the fact that Doctors of the Church and theologians allocate two guardian angels to people who have a position in government—one for the person and another for the office.

From the middle ages on, Catholic theology has taught that every human being, regardless of race, age or sex, has a guardian angel to look after him. There are no exceptions. St Thomas Aquinas goes to the logical extreme by saying that even the Antichrist will be safeguarded by a guardian angel,[2] to prevent him from doing as much harm as he would like to, given his hatred of God. Similarly, we may suppose that persecutors of the Church and enemies of Christianity, such as Hitler or Stalin or the torturers of Dachau or Buchenwald, would have commited even greater crimes were it not for the hidden intervention of their angels. Does it not often happen that a delay, forgetfulness or sickness prevents a crime? It is easy for the angels to arrange this type of thing. They can upset someone's health without any bother.

Guardian angels and the salvation of non-Christians

The invisible but active presence of a guardian angel beside every single one of us invites us to reflect more deeply on the question of the eternal salvation of non-Christians—the pagans of old, as well as contemporary pagans. 'God desires all men to be saved and to come to the knowledge of the truth' (1 Tim 2:4). The Word is the true light 'that enlightens every man' (Jn 1:8). Now, in order to enlighten the human mind God uses not only educators and teachers but also angels. Angels are a standard channel for the transmission of truth.

The Greeks and the Romans gave great importance to inspiration and the role of the muses in poetry. Socrates rendered homage to the help he got from his 'demon', his good genie. Aristotle guessed that superior people benefit from the action of a principle external to human reason; St Thomas Aquinas underlined the same thing in his treatise on the gifts of the Holy Spirit.[4]

As Fr Charles Boulogne notes, the creators of great masterpieces in art and literature, in all periods, realized that they owed their achievement to special powers which they may not have indentified very accurately. 'The authors of these works always recognized that their origin lay in a distant source, higher than their own spirit. When shaping them they all realized that "it had been given to them", they had been inspired. Composers, painters, poets, sculptors, philosophers, mystics—they all knew they been "visited" . . . Some spoke of their *daimon*, others of their "god", and Christians—more clear-sighted—spoke of being helped by God who, in order to reach souls, often uses angels, who are his ministers. Should we not accept their testimony? Their very works of art prove it.'[5]

Vatican Council II recognized that non-Christian religions, such as Hinduism, Buddhism and Islam, contain parts of the truth, reflections of the Word. 'The Catholic Church rejects nothing which is true and holy in these religions. She looks with sincere respect upon those ways of conduct and of life, those rules and teachings which, though differing in many particulars from what she holds and sets forth, nevertheless often reflect a ray of that Truth which enlightens all men.'[6] These rays of truth which enlighten all men as a matter of course are spread with the help of angels, according to St Thomas.

Thus, the teaching of the Church on the protection of angels which all of us enjoy, without exception, throws light on the doctrine of 'sufficient grace'—the doctrine that everyone is granted grace enough to be saved: the lights the angels bring are a concrete expression of sufficient grace. St Thomas states in *De Veritate*: 'It is proper to divine Providence to provide everyone with what is necessary for salvation, provided that the person does not raise obstacles. It could happen that someone grows up in the wild, in the middle of wolves; if he follows the line of conduct his natural reason dictates, seeking good and avoiding evil, it is certain that God will reveal to him, by inward inspiration, everything that it is necessary to believe, or will direct him to a preacher of the faith, just as he sent Peter in search of Cornelius.'[7] Following this teaching, in the case proposed this inward light regarding those things he has to believe normally reaches a person through the intervention of his angel, just as it is by the mystery of angels that someone receives the gift of tongues or of prophecy. 'God has not chained his power to the sacraments.' The non-Christian who, though invincibly ignorant of Revelation, still lives an honest and upright life, can be saved outside the confines of the visible Church.

'You will tread on the lion and the adder'

How do angels go about fulfilling their mission in our daily life? 'He will give his angels charge of you to guard you in all your ways. On their hands they will bear you up, lest you dash your foot against a stone. You will tread on the lion and the adder, the young lion and the serpent you will trample under foot' (Ps 91:11-13).

How do guardian angels intervene in homes, schools, factories, cinemas, parliaments, on the highway, in the air? Can these incorporeal beings actually influence social and professional life, politics, etc? Do they exercise any real, substantial influence in a person's life? Have they a role to play in the history of mankind?

St Thomas Aquinas discovers the answer to these questions by investigating the very nature of the angels. Their knowledge of the natural universe and its laws is incomparably superior to ours. They hold a mysterious power over the material world; their dominion goes way beyond the limits of science and technology— to the extent that some things the angels do seem to us to be miraculous when in fact they are purely natural. We can see parallels to this in our own experience:[8] people in a tribe in the middle of nowhere, completely cut off from the rest of the world, would think it was a miracle if they saw an aeroplane land or heard a transistor radio. Yet there is nothing miraculous about these machines: their makers have an advantage over the tribesmen simply because they know much more about nature and its laws.

In this connection we might look at an episode in the Acts of the Apostles. After being shipwrecked, St Paul and his companions land on Malta. A fire is lit. Paul gathers some firewood and throws it on the fire. A viper jumps out and fastens on to Paul's hand. The Apostle shakes the reptile off into the fire and suffers no harm. The natives expect him to swell up or fall down dead. They watch him for a while and when they see that nothing happens to him they change their attitude. 'He is a god', they exclaim (Acts 28:6).

The islanders regard this stranger's immunity as something miraculous. They take him for a god. But it is very possible that the Apostle was protected because his angel acted on the viper— just as one might attribute to angels the mood of the hungry lions in the pit where Darius had thrown Daniel. 'O King', Daniel said, 'God sent his angel and shut the lions' mouths, and they have not hurt me . . .' (Dan 6:23).

God keeps his promises
Again, there is nothing strange about this to someone who belives in the word of God. The angels' power over the animal world is much greater than that of lion-tamers and snake-charmers. God himself says in one of the psalms, as we have seen, that his chosen ones will tread on serpents and even trample lions under foot (Ps 91:13). A Doctor of the Church tells us that these words should be taken in a literal sense as well as in a spiritual sense[9] and that the same applies to the words 'On their hands [the angels] will bear you up, lest you strike your foot against a stone.'

A person meets physical obstacles and visible enemies in his life and he also experiences moral difficulties and comes up against 'the spiritual hosts of wickedness in the heavenly places' (Eph 6:12).

The guardian angel has been given the job of helping man in all these situations. He can help him at a physical level, lifting him up, keeping at bay some dangerous animal or thing, drawing his attention to danger by means of a noise, etc; similarly, he can intervene at a psychic level—giving his protégé an inspiration or affecting his enemies, making them lose their cover or distracting their attention or inhibiting them in some way.[10]

There are lots of examples we could quote from lives of the saints. It is true that many of them go back to times when people did not have a very scientific approach to investigating alleged events of this kind. There are some people nowadays who question the authenticity of angelic interventions—for example, the authenticity of the voices which inspired St Joan of Arc.

Rather than present here a series of historical facts which could illustrate the verses of Psalm 91 which I have just quoted, I prefer to emphasize two points—1) the assurances which God has given us, and 2) angels' power over the material universe in general and over man's soul in particular.

A believer could perhaps question the authenticity of the appearances of angels to St Frances of Rome, St Lydwine of Schiedam, St Wenceslas, Duke of Bohemia or, closer in time to us, St Gemma Galgani (1878-1903); but, only at the risk of parting company with his faith can he question God's faithfulness in keeping his promises. World leaders can prove false to solemn undertakings they have given; they can violate treaties; but God is faithful. When he makes a promise, he keeps it. There are very many places in holy Scripture where he commits himself to surround his children with protection by angels. Those spiritual beings who have such power over the material universe and over the devil's cohorts. He keeps his promises! Countless saints and fervent Christians have experienced the truth of this.

'You are amazed that your guardian angel has done you such obvious favours. And you should not be amazed: that's why our Lord has placed him beside you' (Blessed J. Escrivá).[11]

Questioning the role of the angels would amount to denying implicitly God's truthfulness and his faithfulness to the promises he has made. It would be a form of blasphemy.[12]

Bringing God down to our level
It might be objected that Catholics today no longer believe in these stories of angels and that the best thing to do is to interpret certain biblical texts in a different way, in order to adapt them to the more mature outlook of modern man.

Firstly, we must point out that there is an exaggeration here: it is only *a part* of the Catholic world, not the whole of it, that is questioning the traditional interpretation of certain biblical texts. Those who think this way are probably far fewer than they appear to be: it is simply that they are more vocal and better organized. Not so long ago a very small group of French lay people got tens of thousands of signatures for a document in support of the pope. Who would have expected it? The same thing happens with Catholics who 'question' the existence of angels, or with priests who 'question' priestly celibacy: alongside a few hundred noisy voices clamouring for change there are thousands and tens of thousands of priests who actively accept celibacy, through silent self-surrender to God.

As regards the core of the matter, that is, the interpretation of sacred Scripture, it may well be that people too often forget that truth revealed by God should not be brought down to our level and adapted to our tastes by all sorts of clever interpretations: rather, we Christians, by an act of faith, need to rise up to the level of divine truths.

People's outspoken opinions cannot be a sounder standard than God's truthfulness. Are shifting sands a better foundation than rock? In the last analysis what matters is not 'what people think' or what they are willing to settle for, but what God thinks and what through Revelation he proposes to us, asking us to believe it. Supernatural truths have to be discovered: they cannot be invented.

There are certain adaptations and interpretations of the Word of God which amount to nothing less than betrayal—inspired though they are by a desire to make Revelation acceptable to a world dazzled by the progress of science and fascinated by the wonders of technology.

In his address at the beginning of the Second Vatican Council, Pope John XXIII made a clear distinction between the unchangeable substance of the truths revealed by God and taught by the Church, and the way these truths are expressed, which ought to be adapted to the different forms of civilization.[13]

In addition to forgetting about God's truthfulness, Christians who are calling in question the existence of guardian angels also seem to forget God's omnipotence. There are many passages in sacred Scripture where the Lord says his power is much greater than men's. 'What is impossible with men is possible with God' (Lk 18:27). God's omnipotence is no myth. A Christian dominated by that 'spirit of technology' denounced by Pius XII and Paul VI may have some difficulty in this connection, but someone endowed with a virile faith can take it in his stride. He can say with St Paul: 'I know whom I have believed' (2 Tim 1:12) and with St John: 'If we receive the testimony of men, the testimony of God is greater' (1 Jn 5:9).

A clear-thinking Catholic will have no difficulty in choosing between writers and preachers who have parted company with the tradition and the teaching authority of the Church on this subject, and the saints and doctors and the liturgy which affirm the existence of angels. He will realize that the authority of theologians and exegetes is not superior to or on a par with the Magisterium: it is on a level below it.[14]

A strategic position

Angels play a protective role as regards the material side of our lives: but seemingly they also play a similar role in our psychic life.[15] They influence our imagination, our memory and our senses, by means of sense images and movements, in order to enlighten us and keep us away from evil and lead us towards good.

An angel cannot directly influence our mind or our will: these faculties are inaccessible to him; only God can reach that far. Angels—both good and bad angels—have free access to our imagination, memory and senses, but can go no further than that. Of course, they can influence our will and intellect in an indirect way by presenting them with material they can work on.[16]

Does this mean that angels have a negligible influence on our mind? Not at all. All we have to do is realize the impact that images, sensations and feelings have on our behaviour: they occupy a very strategic position. While they do not coerce our will in its choice, they do exercise very considerable influence on it. This influence is decisive when the person in question is not very clear-minded or strong-willed, when he is not good at unmasking seduction (by images and feelings) when it occurs. Insight of this sort is the patrimony of an 'elite'. According to St Thomas, 'the majority of men follow the direction in which their senses lead them'. They are at the mercy of sense-images, feelings and passions.

Experience bears this out: in the case of children and even many adults is it not true that all that's needed is for something to glitter—a sweet, a toy, a film, a meeting, some entertainment—for them to feel a strong or even irresistible desire? Look at the influence of films, radio and television: these means of social communication act on our imagination and feelings which in turn influence our minds and wills.

If we ignore the impact of sense-images and feelings in everyday life this could lead us to underestimate the influence of angels, good and bad, on our personal conduct and on the destiny of peoples. But if we do not recognize the influence of images and feelings, then we will more readily grasp the Church's mind in relation to the role of the guardian angels and the role of devils in the spiritual life and in the history of salvation.

A sudden increase in intelligence

The activity of angels seems to have been one of Thomas Aquinas' favourite subjects. In honour of his secretary, Reginald of Priverno, he wrote a treatise on angels (*De substantiis separatis*). He makes mention of angels in the prayers he composed; he frequently refers to them in his *Summa Theologiae* and his *Summa Philosophiae*. He recognizes what he owes them on earth[17] and he rejoices in the thought of one day enjoying their company for ever in heaven. His familiar relationship with them led him to marvellous discoveries. The guardian angels, he writes in his first great work, teach us by lighting up our sense-images, and strengthen the light of our intelligence, leading us to see everything more clearly.[18] Later, he goes into the subject in greater detail, demonstrating that, like a skilled teacher, an angel strives to compose and arrange sense-images in such a way as to give the mind better information to work on.[19] He also emphasizes the mysterious way contact with an angel fortifies a person's mind.[20]

A contemporary French mystic, endowed with an exceptionally clear mind, analyses in these terms the hidden radiation that comes from contact with one's guardian angel: 'When the soul is at one with the angels, she experiences, as it were, a heightening of her faculties. An astronomer when he looks through a telescope discovers horizons which his unaided sight cannot reach. The effect produced in the soul is more or less analogous to this when, through the spiritual contact which unites her to the angel, she experiences a sudden extension of her mind and of her love.'[21]

A growth in one's faculties, and extension of one's mind and will—this is the way the mystic describes it; St Thomas speaks of an enlightening of the mind: both these observations mean the same thing, both speak of the guardian angels exercising a profound influence, although it is difficult to say exactly how this comes about.

If 'in this life we cannot grasp the nature of the angels', obviously we cannot know much about how they operate. We are in the presence of a mystery which invites us, not to suspend our research or our contemplation, but to renounce that hidden pride which desires to understand everything and explain everything.

64

Their closeness to us gives us strength

Using comparisons taken from everyday life, a contemporary theologian describes the secret radiation of angels on people who are open to the truth and to goodness.

'As St Thomas observes, the mere proximity of the angel, the mere fact of being in touch with him, are sufficient to make us better people. The saint teaches that by orientating themselves towards the lower angels or towards human souls, and by coming closer to them, heavenly spirits give them strength, communicating to them something of their own perfection. Fire radiates heat and spreads it around; a flame spreads light; the movement of a solid object thrown into water spreads in extending circles to the edge. In the same way contact with a virtuous person makes us better people. If we come close to a saint, even if we do not converse with him, we feel a kind of encouragement towards virtue, towards goodness, towards holiness.

'In the same way the world of spirits radiates warmth, light and virtue. From it emanates a mysterious, intimate, profound breeze, like a spiritual exhalation, which communicates qualities and perfections.

'How could we not receive some of this from that heavenly spirit who is always by our side? Along with all the most prominent theologians we can believe, therefore, that the nearness of these spirits strengthens us, purifies us, makes us in all sorts of ways better than we would otherwise be.

'This beneficial influence becomes almost visible and palpable in the lives of saints. If they, although they are made like other people and are subject to the same passions, the same miseries, are raised to a quasi-angelic perfection', should this progress also not be attributed to the influence of their angel?[22]

Influencing things via sense-images, intensification of the mind's stength via a mysterious kind of contact—this is, as Fr Legrand puts it, 'the intentional action exercised by angels on man's intellect'.[23]

But, when we receive from the angel this increase in intellectual power, is it not inevitable that we realize what this power is to which we are subject, what the source is of this largesse?

'No', Fr Legrand replies with St Thomas, 'we do not necessarily have here personal communication from one spirit to another, for when a person is enlightened by the action of angels, he may not realize it; he may very well think that he has been the object of a happy accident.[24] A person receives the light and benefits from it, without realizing that his intellectual vigour or the ease with which he grasps the intelligibility of things is the result of angelic cooperation; for there to be spiritual communication in the proper sense of the term the recipient needs to realize that he is receiving "a message" from someone else, and that that message is the result of that other person's personal initiative. But that is not what happens in the case of the human person when he has the good fortune to make a discovery.'[25]

Like a sponge absorbing drops of water

In this connection, St Thomas poses an objection: 'Whoever receives enlightenment is aware of being enlightened. Now men are not directly aware of being enlightened by angels. Therefore they are not enlightened by them.' There we have it: in the hey-day of the Middle Ages, questions are asked about whether guardian angels act on the human spirit.

St Thomas finds the solution to this difficulty by distinguishing enlightenment which one is aware of, and the source of that enlightenment, who is not apparent.[26]

People see a film without seeing the projectionist, but no one would conclude that there *is* no projectionist. He is present, but invisible. From the fact that one's eyes see the fruit on a tree, without seeing the roots of the tree below the ground, no one would conclude that the fruit is the invention of a garderner. The same thing applies to enlightenment which angels effect: the illuminination is apparent, but its source is not.

It is true that sometimes it is very difficult to identify the origin of the images which run around inside us. Some of them are obviously connected with thoughts and sensations which came earlier. Others, connected with our past, seem to arise from our subconscious. How can we recognize those which come from angels, whether good angels or bad angels?

In his *Spiritual Exercises* St Ignatius Loyola gives some very precise rules for discerning inspirations from good angels and temptations by bad angels. The former bring serenity and peace to the soul, whereas the second cause worry and uneasiness.

We shall quote here the seventh rule, which explains that, depending on the moral dispositions of the person concerned, the influence of angels is sometimes very obvious, sometimes very subtle. 'When souls are advancing from good to better, the touch of the good angels is soft, light and gentle, like a drop of water falling on a stone. But their action is the opposite with those who are going from bad to worse. The reason is that the state of the soul is either contrary or similar to these angels. When it is contrary, they make their way in with perceptible noise and sensation; when it is similar, they come in quietly, like a man coming into his own house when the door is open.'[27]

Some people who are particularly alert can sense whether this or that idea has come to them from outside. They are being very accurate when they say in these situations that they are inspired. Similar experiences are to be found even among people who have no contact with the Christian tradition.[28]

Angels can come and go as they please inside people's imagination and feelings—but always must stay within God's scheme of things. An angel can come and go as he pleases, day or night, during work or rest, in the middle of a noisy crowd or in the peace of solitude. A man, on the contrary, does not have the same scope to influence others. He cannot go out and meet them wherever they may be; he cannot enter into communication with them in a flash. A girl sometimes has to wait weeks and months before she sees her boyfriend; a parent may only with difficulty see a child who is away in boarding-school. But it is different with the guardian angels. They can be continuously in touch with their protégé. For them there are no delays, no distances, no separations. This nearness has an advantage, to which Pope John XXIII referred when he said that via our guardian angels we can at any time establish communication with one another.

This may not seem very important—but it is if we think about it: it has a very practical value for human relationships, whether of friendship, education, apostolate, diplomacy or even politics.

'Address my guardian angel'

As we saw earlier, before meeting von Beseler, the governor of Warsaw, the future Pius XI, then apostolic visitor to Poland, successfully pressed into service the general's guardian angel.

We have also seen how Pius XI, drawing on his own experience, advized Monsignor Roncalli, then apostolic visitor to Bulgaria, to seek the mediation of the guardian angels before engaging in difficult negotiations.

When he was going up into the pulpit, St Francis de Sales used pause to look around at the people present: when doing so he was greeting their guardian angels, asking them to make his listeners well-disposed to him. St Paul of the Cross, the founder of the Passionists, had the same custom.

'When you are in need of my prayer, address my guardian angel through your own angel', Padre Pio used to say to his friends. Lots of examples could be given of this hidden diplomacy. When their protégés are people who 'seek first the kingdom of God and his justice', the guardian angels prove to be very reliable and efficient messengers.

A busload of pilgrims en route to San Giovanni Rotondo, where Padre Pio lived, was caught at night in a violent storm in the Apennines mountains. After the first few moments of panic— there was a lot of lightning—the pilgrims recalled Padre Pio's advice and prayed to his angel. They came through unharmed. The following day, before they had a chance to tell him about their journey, Padre Pio forestalled them, smiling: 'Well, my children, last night you woke me up and I had to pray for you ...' The angel guardian had faithfully carried out his mission, bringing to the monastery the SOS sent out from the mountains some miles away.

A mother cannot always directly influence a son or daughter whose faith or moral conduct is at risk, but at any time of the day or night she can use the invisble communication network of the guardian angels. An angel, mobilized by his mother, can suddenly remind a young man of some resolution or promise. And this reminder can be of decisive importance. Sometimes it takes very little to influence an indecisive will. The guardian angels are there precisely to serve men as they make their way towards God.

It is true that angels cannot take over the people they protect: that would undermine the order established by God who wants everyone to make the fullest use of his freedom; but they do want to help man in all situations where he finds himself at a disadvantage. It doesn't matter whether his inadequacy is barely noticeable or, on the contrary, absolutely obvious. 'Our guardian angel's desire to help us,' says St John Bosco, 'is much greater than our desire to be helped by him.'[29]

In reply to her judges, who had asked whether the angels who appeared to her wore any clothes, St Joan of Arc gave this answer, full of human and Christian wisdom: 'Do you think that God has not enough material to dress his angels?' The same kind of answer might be given to Christians who doubt the power of the angels

68

and do not realize they can seek their aid: 'Do you think that God has not the resources to equip angels to perform their mission among men?'

Scattering largesse

There are two other difficulties which prevent Christians from trusting in their angel guardians.

First objection: 'Why complicate life? Why bring in this mediation by angels? Why not link man directly with God? Would that not be much simpler?'

It is true that God could have done without the assistance of angels. In an instant he could demobilize the myriad angels who currently operate on earth and take over himself the work they do—among Christians, Moslems, Buddhists, among believers and atheists.

If he were to do that, his omnipotence and 'self-reliance' would shine out—but his love would not be so obvious. Love wants to spread itself out, in the way the sun tends to diffuse light. Love leads God to give himself without measure, in all areas. The creative power of love extends from the material world to the spiritual world: it embraces the countless stars of the Milky Way and the countless angels in heaven. As St Thomas points out, God's love does not limit itself to giving existence and life to creatures: it goes further and confers on creatures the dignity of being causes.[30] God's love gives a flower the capacity to produce seeds, which are the germs of future flowers; it gives man and woman the ability to transmit life to other human beings. God associates priests in his work of spreading revealed truth and supernatural life throughout the world. In the same way, he associates angels in his work of governing the universe.

Because he cannot do things all by himself, a leader gets people to assist him; out of his superabundance of resources God associates the angels in the government of the world and confers on them the dignity of being causes. Man has too little; God has infinitely too much, if we may put it that way—and to spread himself he creates guardian angels and uses them to distribute his largesse.

Undoubtedly this kind of behaviour can disconcert people who use man's ruler to measure the things of God. But it ceases to be surprising when we approach things with the great insight that faith confers: 'For my thoughts are not your thoughts, neither are your ways my ways, says the Lord. For as the heavens are higher than the earth, so are my ways higher than your ways and my thoughts than your thoughts (Is 55:8-9).

Source and channel

The second difficulty has to do with the relationship between God and the guardian angel in the help that men are given. Are God and the angel in some way independent of each other, do they work independently? Is there some kind of competition or rivalry between them, so they avoid both doing the same thing? Is the guardian angel like an ambassador who is tempted to exceed his brief? If the protection given by the angel consists principally in enlightening the mind of his protégé, where does the Holy Spirit fit in in connection with inspirations from on high? In other words, why complicate things by bringing mediation by angels?

The truth of the matter is that there is no rivalry, no competition, no opposition involved between the guardian angels and God. There is, rather, cooperation—the same sort of cooperation as obtains between central government on the one hand and provincial government, which carries out its orders. God is the source of all graces; some of these reach souls directly, others through the angels. There are graces which God gives people directly because these graces cannot be 'administered' by angels. There are some jobs a priest can leave to lay people, but he cannot depute them to hear confessions or celebrate Mass: these sacred duties are beyond lay people. Similarly, to reach the core of man's soul is beyond the power of an angel. To do that, God has to intervene personally.

Two things are required for an action to be good, St Thomas explains: first, we must want to be good (this is induced by training in moral virtue); second, reason must discover suitable means to achieve good (this is the task of prudence). With regard to the first, God helps man directly by infusing graces and virtues; with regard to the second, God helps man indirectly through the ministry of angels, who are channels of God's lights.[31]

God is lord of all and guardian of all, and he also acts through subordinate lords and guardians who carry out his orders. God works at the top of the pyramid, the angels cooperate with him at lower levels. There is no question of competition or opposition: angels *cooperate* with God.

The masters of the spiritual life insist on this distinction. They stress the superiority of those gifts conferred directly by God on

70

souls, while also emphasizing that the lights angels give us are also of divine origin. Good thoughts originate with God, but they come to us through the ministry of angels.[32] The channel is a tributary of the source.[33]

Not just near us, but in us
The angel does not give us compunction of heart, St Bonaventure says, but he does show us where to find it. And he reminds us of the words of the psalm: 'He (God) heals our contrite hearts' (Ps 147:3).[34] It is God himself who either fills our souls with light, St Bernard says, or visits us through his angels, or instructs us by means of men or consoles us by means of the Scriptures.[35] 'The angels and archangels are here and they render us aid', he writes to his disciple, who later became Pope Eugene III. 'But He who causes the seed which they have planted to grow within us is He who is not only near us but in us. If you tell me that the angel can also be in us, I will not disagree with you, because I remember that it is written "The angel who spoke in me said."[36] But there is a great difference. The angels are in us through the good thoughts they suggest to us and not by virtue of the good they work in our soul. They exhort us to goodness, but they do not create goodness in us. Whereas God is in us in such a way that he directly affects our soul, pours his gifts into her, or better, it is He himself who pours himself into our soul and makes us sharers in his divinity. The angels are with our soul, but God is inside our soul. The angels dwell under the same roof as our soul, but God is with her as her very life.'[37]

According to St John of the Cross, the predominance of God's direct intervention in the soul, without the mediation of the guardian angels, is what characterizes the higher stages of the spiritual life. 'It is characteristic of this union of the soul with God (in the spiritual marriage) that God works in her and communicates himself to her alone, not now by means of angels, as aforetime, neither by means of her natural ability.'[38]

God at this stage communicates himself to the soul 'without other means—either of angels, or men, or images, or forms'. 'The outward and inward senses, and all creatures, and even the soul herself, have very little to do with the receiving of these great and supernatural favours which God grants in this state.'[39]

St Thomas' teaching on charisms throws light on this distinction. Charisms—such as, for example, the gift of tongues, discernment of spirits, prophecy—have an essentially social purpose: the soul receives them not in order to increase her spiritual life but for the instruction and guidance of others. Charisms are attributed to the Holy Spirit inasmuch as he is a first principle, Thomas says; nevertheless they reach men through the mediation of the angels.[40]

Nothing to surprise a Christian

The history of the Church in our times shows us two people who were richly endowed with gifts—Theresa Neumann, the stigmatist of Konnersreuth, and Padre Pio of San Giovanni Rotondo. Many people bear witness that the Capuchin stigmatist, in the confessional, understood foreign languages which he did not know and read the secrets of hearts, to the point of sometimes completing the confessions of some penitents: 'You have not confessed such and such a sin, committed in such and such circumstances...' It is also well known that Padre Pio followed the advice of Pius XII: he had a constant, close relationship with his guardian angel.[41] God made use of this visible intermediacy to reveal sins and states of soul to Padre Pio, and to enable him to understand foreign languages.

Theresa Neumann had a similar familiar relationship with her guardian angel; she too had amazing gifts. 'Theresa, in her normal state, continuously sees a man of light, an angel, on her right hand side (as she sees other people's angels also on their right hand side) and holds continuous conversation with him. This angel reveals to her whatever she need know about the hidden life or state of soul of her visitors ... What sometimes is taken for an intuitive knowledge of souls ... and of which so many examples are quoted, is in her case really the result of a revelation, which is something completely different.'[42] She knew with complete certainty whether her visitors or the people she saw in the crowd had recently been to Communion.[43]

Things like this, which are well documented, may disconcert a non-believer, but there is no reason why they should surprise a Christian. A Christian knows that God is love, a love burning to share his graces, and that normally he does this in cooperation with the angels.

If the angel guardians bring gifts to the soul, do they play a part in communicating the gifts of the Holy Spirit? Here we must make a distinction. While certain gifts directly affect the intelligence (the gift of wisdom) or the will (the gift of fortitude), others (counsel, knowledge) concern the discursive reason which sifts data from the exterior and interior senses. It would seem therefore, that some gifts of the Holy Spirit reach the soul without any intermediary, whereas others come indirectly, through the mediation of angels.

No strikes, no holidays

'He will give his angels charge over you to guard you in all your ways' (Ps 91:11). This verse of Holy Scripture, like other biblical texts, is very deep and becomes clear only gradually, through contemplation.

If we say that angels guard us 'in all our comings and goings', does this not amount to saying that their watchfulness extends over our whole life, from infancy through adulthood to old age, day and night, at work and at rest, in the fleeting times of joy and the never-ending times of sorrow?

People get three, four, five or more weeks of holiday per year. The guardian angels take no holidays. They are always on the job. They work twenty-four hours a day. In order to win better conditions people sometimes down tools; the guardian angels never go on strike. From the moment a human being sees the light of day until when, as child, adult or elderly person, he breathes his last before appearing in God's presence, his angel guardian is at his side, year in year out, month in month out, day in day out, hour in hour out: he is never away for a moment.[44]

Looked at from the viewpoint of either protector or protégé, the reasons for this constant presence are obvious. God has ordained that his angels should guard man in all his comings and goings. Well, angels would never disobey even in the slightest thing. They do not know infidelity, casualness, inconsistency, forgetfulness, absence—things which are quite common among men. 'Bless the Lord, all you angels of the Lord, sing his glory and praise for ever,' the psalmist prays. The Church includes these verses in the Mass of the Guardian Angels.

The angels see God continually, Jesus tells us. Their guardianship is nothing other than a consequence of this uninterrupted contemplation. The sight of God and the guardianship of men are, for them, one and the same activity.

This basic and permanent perfection which is to be found in the guardian angels contrasts with men's congenital and continuous imperfection. Without relaxing for a moment, the devil is lying in wait to separate man from God. The continual presence of evil calls for continual presence of its remedy, just as a permanent state of siege means one must be continually on the defensive. A commander-in-chief will not demobilize his troops as long as the enemy is lined up on the frontier. A doctor does not leave his patients, as long as they are still sick.

Every man, woman and child

There is a third aspect to the protection angels give us. It extends not only throughout history and throughout the world: it covers everything people do.

Body and soul, shelter, dress, food and living conditions, health, activities of the spirit, work and prayer: everything which concerns men concerns their angels.

As numerous episodes in sacred Scripture remind us, angels show their care for us even in things which we might think unimportant or rather beneath a 'prince of the heavenly court', such as bringing food to an exhausted prophet in the desert, curing an old man blinded by a bird's droppings, or taking an active part in a defensive war (the Maccabees). The sacred writer also gives us many examples of how angels stoop to very humble aspects of men's existence.

These heavenly spirits do not in any way despise what some people might call menial tasks, for nothing that is ordained to God's service and to the service of men whom God loves is unworthy in their eyes. From the moment that any activity in itself good is orientated towards God, St Thomas says, that activity 'is divinized' in some way. No matter how unimportant it might appear, it is raised high, away above nobler occupations performed with purely human outlook. When she went about housework in her house in Nazareth, Mary was doing something infinitely higher, morally speaking, than an arrogant king presiding over the destinies of an empire.

Knowing God, loving him and serving him, loving all men for God's sake—this is the purpose of all human life, and the guardian angels' entire effort is in the same direction. But is prayer not the greatest means available to man to achieve this elevation to God?

Their presence in man's worship of God

It is easy to perceive the capital role angels play in the official prayer of the Church and in personal prayer.

Erik Peterson, Cardinal Daniélou and Dom Cipriano Vaggagini have done a lot of research into 'this aspect of liturgical life which is so forgotten and so little known'.

The insertion of the public and private prayer of the faithful into the liturgy of the angels, and the presence of the angels in the worship which men render God—this especially merits our attention, because it is something which is so often missed, even by Christians who are very involved in the liturgical renewal decreed by Vatican II. It is too often forgotten that the angels, contemplating, as they do, the face of God, are adorers *par excellence*. They are the masters of liturgy.

The entire worship offered by the Church on earth is in fact a sharing in the worship which the angels and the elect render God in heaven: each has the same object, God, and the same spiritual impulse, Christ, the head of the Mystical Body. This thesis derives not only from Holy Scripture but also from the Tradition of the Church and from the liturgical texts themselves.

'There is only one priestly activity', Cardinal Daniélou explains, 'and that is Jesus Christ's. By it the whole of creation glorifies the Trinity. This is the same activity that is offered by the angels in heaven and the saints on earth. This participation appears in the New Testament, where the liturgy of the Church is presented as a participation in that of the angels. Thus, in the Epistle to the Hebrews 12:22-24, we read: "But you have come to Mount Sion, and to the city of the living God, the heavenly Jerusalem, and to the company of many thousands of angels . . . and to a sprinkling of blood which speaks better than Abel." As for the Apocalypse, it is the vision of the Christian Sunday worship that the visionary sees as prolonged in the liturgy of heaven.'[45]

Speaking of the sacrifice of the Mass, Daniélou points out how 'the display of the liturgy on earth is a visible reflection, an efficacious symbol, of the heavenly liturgy of the angels. This unity of the two cults is expressed by the liturgy itself in the Preface, where it invites the community of the Church to unite with the Thrones and the Dominations, the Cherubim and the Seraphim, to sing the angelic hymn of praise, the Thrice-Holy, the *Trisagium*.'[46]

'Reflect on whom you have at your side and with whom you are going to invoke God,' St John Chrysostom exhorts us,[47] '—with the Cherubim themselves. Just imagine the choirs you are going to join. Let no one neglect to join in these mystical and sacred hymns. Let no one be distracted by profane thoughts (*Sursum corda!*), but rather, detaching yourselves from all earthly things and transporting yourself entirely to heaven, like one who is beside the very throne of glory and flying among the Seraphim, sing the holy hymn of the God of glory and of majesty.'

Commenting on the letter to the Colossians (3:8), the holy Doctor observes: the catechumens may take part in the Mass up to the *Gloria in excelsis Deo*, the canticle of the lower orders of angels, whereas the *Sanctus*, the canticle of the Seraphim, is reserved to the initiated, the baptized.

Dom C. Vaggagini points to an interesting connection between the Trisagium of the Seraphim, included in the Preface of the Mass, and the third petition of the Our Father, in which Christ teaches men to imitate on earth the behaviour of the angels in heaven. 'The triple acclamation of the word "Holy", which according to Isaiah the Seraphim alternate in prayer to God, was used by the Hebrews in the Synagogue liturgy, and was termed *Kedushah*, that is to say, the "hallowing", hallowing of the name of God. There is nothing surprising in its passing from Jewish usage to the prayer of the early Christians: for in the Lord's prayer itself they every day pray God may be "hallowed" on earth as he is hallowed by the angels in heaven.'[48]

Using a penetrating piece of exegesis by Origen, which is supported by recent studies of the Qumran art of poety, and applying also the interpretation given in the catechism of the Council of Trent, a contemporary biblical scholar, Fr Jean Carmignac, is of the view that the words 'on earth as it is in heaven', that is to say, 'by men as by angels in heaven', applies to each of the first three petitions of the Our Father, not just to the third petition as is commonly believed.'[49] Thus, Jesus exhorts his disciples to follow the example of the angels in their hallowing of the 'name of God, in their work to promote the coming of his kingdom and the fulfilment of his will'.

Daniélou, Vaggagini and Peterson cite other texts in which the same idea occurs—the liturgy of men on earth is connected with the liturgy of the angels in heaven. There is nothing strange in this, because, as St Thomas Aquinas points out, 'men and angels have a common purpose, which is the glory of enjoying God. Hence, the mystical body of the Church is made up of angels as well as men'.[50] It is like an orchestra made up of an infinite number of players: some sing, some play instruments, all have a single purpose, all come under the one conductor, Christ. 'Because Christ causes grace in the members he is called head of the Church.'[51]

And that is not all. The guardian angels, who have the mission of helping us in all our physical, intellectual and spiritual activities, would not be faithful to their task if they did not, so to speak, devote their best energies to stimulating and supporting the most necessary, the noblest, activity of their protégés—the worship of God, which can take the form of adoration, atonement, thanksgiving and petition.

St John Chrysostom does everything he can to get his people to realize the angels are invisibly present during the Holy Sacrifice: 'The angels surround the priest; the sanctuary and especially the altar are peopled by heavenly hosts, in honour of him who is up on the altar.'[52] And to expand on this statement, which emanates from his faith, the saint adds, by way of sharing a confidence: 'in a vision angels have been seen, surrounding the altar, bowing to the ground, as guards bow to the King.' St Thomas says the same: 'our belief is that the angels visit the assembly of the faithful, especially when the sacred mysteries are being celebrated.'[53] 'If the kings of this world are surrounded by their nobles, is it not fitting that the King of kings be surrounded by his court wherever he be?'[54]

Thus, the visible assembly of the faithful is paralleled by an invisible assembly of angels, as Origen explains,[55] commenting on Psalm 34:7: 'The angel of the Lord encamps around those who fear him, and delivers them': 'If the angel of the Lord moves around those who fear him it is probable that, when they are honourably gathered for the glory of the Lord, each person's angel moves around him who fears him and stays with that person whom he has been charged to guard and guide. In such a way that there are two Churches, that of men and that of angels   And so we ought believe that the angels attend the assemblies of believers.'

In St Gregory the Great's view, these truths are not to be questioned: 'What Christian could doubt that at the very hour of the sacrifice the heavens open on hearing the priest's voice, that the choirs of angels are present at this mystery of Jesus Christ, that the higher creatures share their prerogatives with us, that the earthly are united to the heavenly creatures, and that what is visible forms one single thing with what is invisible?'[56]

Religious art bears witness to this presence of the angels in the liturgy by showing angels gathered round the tabernacle, in paintings and sculptures.

This presence of angels imposes respect. Would any well-mannered person act casually or rudely in the presence of an important personality? The presence of angels at private prayer and especially at liturgical acts calls for special behaviour: the norms given by St Paul and St Benedict and the advice given by Tertullian and by the author of the Rule of the Master bear witness to this.

The Apostle of the Gentiles or, to be more exact, the Holy Spirit speaking through him, prescribes that women should keep their heads veiled during the assembly also 'because of the angels', that is to say, out of respect for the angels invisibly present at the act of worship.[57]

As St Clement of Alexandria points out,[58] even when he is praying on his own, man is in the midst of choirs of angels. This is why Tertullian recommends to Christians not to sit while they pray, out of respect 'for the angel of prayer who is by our side.'[59]

St Benedict in his Rule (Chapter 19) echoes these ideas: 'We believe that God is present everywhere but we ought believe it especially, with all firmness, when we attend the divine office.' Psalm 13:1 says 'I will sing to you in the presence of the angels.' From this the Father of western monasticism draws the following conclusion: 'Let us consider what is the best attitude for us to adopt in the presence of God and of the angels and prepare our psalmody in such a way that our spirit harmonizes with our voice.'

A Benedictine monk of the eighth century, Paul the Deacon, comments as follows on this passage in the Rule: 'This norm may be understood in two ways: one, when we sing the psalms to God, the angels are present, for God is never without his heralds; the other, if our heart is attentive to what our mouth says, then, our intention is like that of the angels.' Far from the one excluding the other, do these two meanings not complement each other?

The Rule of the Master (*Regula Magistri*), the work of a spiritual writer of the Middle Ages, shows us the extent to which people at that time had a realistic idea of the presence of the angels at the psalmody of the monks: 'If someone is praying and wants to cough or sneeze, let him be careful not to do it *in front*, but rather behind his back, because of the angels, who are in front of him, since the Prophet tells him: I will sing psalms to you in the presence of the angels.'[60] Being all very modern we might be tempted to smile at this type of thing. It might be better if we respected the refined feelings and vigorous faith which inspired it.

Origen, who also had a very well-developed sense of the presence of angels in our lives, draws a conclusion which is rich in spiritual applications; he uses three biblical texts to throw light on each other. These three texts are: the words of Christ about angels ascending and descending, St Paul's point about women in church, and the episode of Elisha and Gehazi at Dothan: 'It is prescribed that women should be veiled when praying, because of the angels. Which angels? Those who attend the faithful and who rejoice in the Church, and whom we, because our eyes are darkened by the stain of sin, do not see, but the Apostles of Jesus do see them, for to them was it said: "Truly, truly, I say to you, you will see heaven opened, and the angels of God ascending and descending upon the Son of Man" (Jn 1:51). If I had the grace to see like the Apostles, I would perceive the multitude of angels which Elisha saw and which Gehazi, who was at his side, did not see.'[61] Like a telescope pointed out at the immensity of the sky, our faith opens up for us a whole invisible world, which is beyond the reach of the human mind left to its own resources.

He lends them his wings

It is interesting to note that the Church, aware of man's weakness, invites the angels to support her children in their prayer. Such is the difficulty we experience in extracting ourselves from our everyday concerns and becoming recollected! To raise our hearts and spirits above the bustle of life, the angels need to move their wings. In this connection Bossuet observes: 'Do not be alarmed if I ask you to examine your conscience. What an effort it takes to raise up your hearts when you offer God your prayers! What storms surround you when you make your resolutions. How many vain imaginings, how many vague, disordered thoughts, how many temporal occupations get in the way and interrrupt the course of those prayers. Distracted in this way, do you think your prayers can rise up to heaven; can your weak and languid prayer, which meets so many obstacles that it can scarcely leave your heart, have the strength to cross the clouds and penetrate the height of heaven? . . . Could anyone expect it to do so? Surely those prayers would fall by their own weight, if the goodness of God had not provided. . . . He sent his angel, whom Tertullian calls the angel of prayer. This is why Raphael said to Tobias: "I have offered your prayers to God" . . . The angel comes to gather our prayers and "they rise," says St John, "from the hands of the angel to the face of God". . . . See how thy rise from the hands of the angel; think how they are helped by being presented by hands so pure. They rise from the hands of the angel because this angel, by coming to us and helping our feeble prayers, lends them his wings to rise up, his stength to remain raised up, and his fervour to give them life.'[62]

The Church's call on angels for help becomes more dramatic in its prayer for the dying. When a person is dying he feels completely hemmed in: his loss of physical energy can easily drain him also of spiritual energy. The devil uses all his resources to make a last assault to capture a prey before it escapes for ever. Angels of light and angels of darkness confront one another at the bedside of the dying person. It is easy to understand why the Church mobilizes the angels at this moment, so decisive for his eternal destiny.

St Thomas draws a parallel between the influence of angels and that of devils. He rejects the theory which refers every sin to the direct influence of devils. That, he thinks, is going too far: the burden of original sin, aggravated by a person's other faults and by the natural pressure of his passions is strong enough in itself to lead someone to commit sin, without any need to posit that temptation by the devil is at the root of every sin. However, a man's supernatural actions are another matter. These occur on a higher level, which man cannot rise to by his own effort. 'Men cannot advance in merit without God's help which is extended to them through the angels' ministry.' From this mediation by angels, St Thomas draws a conclusion rich in insights for spirituality and for pastoral guidance: 'The angels cooperate in all our good works.'[63]

Pius XI opened up these horizons about the role of the guardian angels in the history of every soul, when he confided to his visitors that his guardian angel had played a part in all the good it had been granted him to do in the course of his life.

They see God

Christians who contemplate and imitate the angels run the risk of meeting up with Pascal's maxim that man is neither angel nor beast, and unfortunately anyone who wants to become an angel, becomes a beast. Are we not entering a dream world—and liable to a rude awakening—if we indulge in intimate conversation with the angels?

This objection has no basis. Pascal is not against contemplation of the world of angels, which is a real world attested to by Revelation. He is, rather, condemning the attitude of people who act as if their soul were independent of their body, that body which Scripture states is subject to corruption and which conditions our spiritual activity: 'For the reasoning of mortals is worthless, and our attempts are likely to fail, for a perishable body weighs down the soul, and this earthly tent burdens the thoughtful mind' (Wis 9:14-15). It should not surprise us that the Church encourages us to admire and imitate the angels. She puts even higher examples before us—our Lady, Christ the God-man, and God himself. If one author has given us *The Imitation of Christ* and another *The Imitation of Mary*, is it surprising to find, in the last century, someone trying to write an *Imitation of the Angels*?

St Thomas Aquinas went in this direction when he dwelt on two characteristics of the guardian angels—their imperturbable serenity in the face of moral and physical evil and the way they perfectly combine action and contemplation. These two characteristics of angels can give us valuable insights for our spiritual life and apostolate.

Are the angels sad?

Given that he is constantly focused on man, to protect him, encourage him and inspire him, is the guardian angel saddened by those things which weigh down his protégé—material loss, professional failures, accidents, illnesses, old age, inconstancy, weaknesses, venial sins and even mortal sins? Given that he accompanies man in all his comings and goings, does the guardian angel not sometimes have reason to be sad? Does his heart, if we may speak in that way, always beat in unison with his protégé's? What is the angel's attitude to that question which secretly torments believers who are ill-instructed, that question which is a stumbling-block to so many non-believers in their search for the truth—the question of evil: natural catastrophes, starving children, incurable disease, the trials of good people, crimes which cry to heaven, the success of evildoers? How does the guardian angel react to the common objection. 'If God existed he would not permit evil; therefore God does not exist'?

Here we are in a dilemma. Either the angel suffers when we suffer material loss or commit sins, and in this case his happiness is not unalloyed; heaven ceases to be heaven for him. Or else our guardian angel does not weep when we weep, he is selfishly indifferent, as cold as a statue; in which case he lacks one of the qualities we most appreciate in our friends—understanding and sympathy.

The solution which St Thomas gives to this apparently insoluble problem provides new insights into the world of the angels and into man's own world.

Angels, the Doctor explains, do not grieve either for sins or for the punishments visited on men. This is the real reason for an angels' serenity: only things which are contrary to an angel's will can cause him pain or sadness. Nothing in the world happens against the will of angels: their will is completely at one with God's, and nothing happens in the world save what is done by, or permitted by, God's justice. Nothing, then, here below can go contrary to the angel's will, because nothing happens which is not included in the plans of Providence.[1]

Why does God permit evil? Because *there is nothing else he can do*? Certainly not. He is almighty. All he would need would be something ridiculously small, like Cromwell's kidney-stone, to control an assassin or a tyrant. He could overpower a Stalin in a flash, as he did with Agrippa I (cf. Acts 12:23). If God tolerates an evil, it is always and only so as to draw some good out of it, sooner or later.

St Thomas explains this policy of God's by giving a very simple example—what a sailor does whose ship, with a full cargo of merchandize, is liable to be wrecked in a storm. In principle and in general the sailor has no desire to throw his cargo overboard; but rather than be shipwrecked he prefers to see it dumped in the

82

sea. His loss—of the cargo—becomes gain—of his boat and his crew. From evil good comes. He sacrifices what is less important, and saves what is more important. He acts wisely. If he obstinately tried to save the cargo, he would lose his ship and his life.[2]

Indifference or wisdom?
God is acting like this when he tolerates sickness and epidemics, earthquakes and floods, crime, war, moral faults, sacrilege, the apostasy of individuals and nations: if he does not prevent these evils, as he easily could do, it is because, at some point or other, his power and wisdom will draw greater good from them.

Out of the dark abyss of human wretchedness, God's mercy is able to draw unsuspected treasure. Angels know this.

So, it is not out of indifference that angels are not saddened by the misfortunes and faults of their protégés: it is because they have a deeper understanding of these events. Their serenity is not based on ignorance, but on superior knowledge. Where we can see only the rough outer shell of misfortunes and calamities, angels can look inside and also see the future. In the grain of seed planted in the ground we can already see the full-grown tree. Angels participate in God's knowledge, and God in a single glance takes in everything—past, present and future.

In a magnificent page, worthy of St Augustine, Pius XII draws a parallel between men's restricted outlook and God's infinite knowledge (in which the angels share). 'Men are but children before God—everyone, even great thinkers, great leaders. They all judge events in a short-sighted way, from the perspective of time, which flies past, never to return, whereas God looks at them from high above, from the unchanging centre of eternity. Men see the narrow panorama of a few years; God sees the complex and mysterious interplay of all responsible beings, his Providence respecting the freedom of every human decision, whether made by good or bad people. Men would like to see instant justice; they are scandalized by the (short-lived) power of God's enemies and by the sufferings and humiliations of the good. But their heavenly Father, in the light of his eternity, embraces, penetrates and governs the vicissitudes of the times, bestowing the serene peace of endless ages; God, the Blessed Trinity, is full of compassion for human weakness, ignorance and impatience; he who loves men too much to let them by their own fault take leave of the paths of wisdom and of his love; he continues and will continue to make the sun rise on the good and the bad, to have the rain fall on the just and the unjust (Mt 5:45), guiding their childish steps firmly and tenderly, asking of them nothing but that they let him lead them and place their trust in the power and in the wisdom of the love he has for them.'[3]

The angel knew

The sons of Jacob cast their brother Joseph into a well and sold him to Egyptian merchants in order to be rid of him: this was a horrible crime, yet God made it produce wonderful results: 'As for you, you meant evil against me,' Joseph would later tell his brothers, when he was prime minister of Egypt, 'but God meant it for good, to bring it about that many people should be kept alive, as they are today' (Gen 50:20). Disapproving of the criminal behaviour of his brothers, Reuben had wanted to save Joseph and return him to his father: he tore his vestments in sorrow when he found his brothers had sold Joseph to Ishmaelites when he was away. Reuben wept, but his angel, like Joseph's, was unperturbed, because he knew God would draw good out of this evil deed.

St John of the Cross was thrown into a dungeon in the monastery at Toledo by some of his confrères—disgraceful behaviour, but God made it lead to wonderful things. It was precisely during his imprisonment that the master of the dark night received those graces which raised him to the highest level of mysticism. After he escaped he referred to his jailers as great benefactors. His intimate union with God enabled him to share, in some way, in that wonderful insight into events which the angels enjoy, inserted as they are in God's plans, an insight which allows them see that if God permits an evil it is only so as to be able to draw a great good from it.

Picture Ignatius Loyola gravely wounded at Pamplona. His friends on earth would have said, 'What a shame! The end of a brilliant army career.' But his friends in heaven would have thought: 'What luck! This means freedom. Now, shaken by grace, Captain Ignatius will begin an incomparably nobler and more useful career than the profession of arms!'

In the same way our guardian angels, the saints in heaven and our dead friends freed from the flames of purgatory and wrapped in God's light, are quite serene when they see the material miseries and moral faults of men.

At first sight this seems inhuman, even monstrous. How can a

MY ANGEL

mother, who is in heaven, not be saddened by the misfortunes of her children still on earth? Does she not feel for their physical needs? Do their sins not cause her suffering? Does she not tremble when she sees them on the road to perdition?

We say it again: the serenity of the citizens of heaven in the face of the evils which afflict people on earth is not the result of ignorance or indifference, as if they were strangers unconcerned about the lot of the people around them. It stems from a more enlightened love, a deeper insight, because their will is completely in tune with God's, whose providential plans nothing on earth can upset; the elect who have already entered the peace of God do not suffer when they see what is happening in the world. Their minds are conformed to God's, and therefore they see in men's misfortunes the development of God's designs, all of which are worthy of worship.[4]

'You will see that everything was good'
After being converted and founding a religious institute, Captain Ignatius Loyola actively cultivated the angels. He wanted to see, in the members of the Society of Jesus, charity, and the zealous and unshakeable serenity of the angels.[5] In his *Spiritual Exercises*, St Ignatius calls the attention of those doing the exercises to the angels; and the Jesuits, faithful to their founder, still spread devotion to the angels.

Another spiritual giant of the sixteenth century, St John of the Cross, asks pious souls to imitate the angels' serenity in the face of evil, especially in the face of their neighbours' sins—instead of indulging in uncontrolled zeal and sterile complaint. The further the soul advances in the spiritual life the more she changes her attitude to her neighbours' faults. First she moves from indifference to severity and restlessness; later she is quite serene and refrains from criticism, though without thereby approving of the evil.

'For the grandeur and stability of the soul in this estate are so complete that, if formerly there reached the soul the waters of any grief soever, even those of its own sins or of the sins of some other person . . . now, although it still realizes their importance, they cause it neither pain nor sorrow . . . for in this transformation of love the soul is made like to the angels, who apprehend perfectly things that are grievous, without feeling grief, and perform works of mercy and compassion without feeling compassion.'[6]

In his wisdom, St Augustine observes that God prefers to draw good out of evil, rather than not allow any evil to occur.[7]

In exactly the same sense, misfortune is preferable to the absence of misfortune, because of what the good God draws out of it. It is like a dark tunnel which opens out into the light. By contemplating everything in God, the angel sees this bright exit, which can easily escape man's short-sightedness.

In an incomparably better way than man, angels grasp the truth of this verse of sacred Scripture: 'in everything God works for good with those who love him' (Rom 8:28). Everything, comments St Augustine—even sins, for they can lead us to distrust ourselves more and trust more fully in God.

Julian of Norwich, in her concern over the problem of evil and suffering, confided in our Lord. He set her mind at ease, inviting her to trust in his love and in his omnipotence: '[But Jesus said]: "It behoved that there should be sin [in this naked word *sin*, our Lord brought to my mind, generally, all that is not good]; but all shall be well, and all shall be well, and all manner of thing shall be well".' Dom Paul Renaudin comments: 'The misery around us and the wretchedness in the very heart of man are nothing but the field of operations of Mercy and Grace; they are an opportunity for Redemption. Have confidence, the world is encompassed and borne up by God's boundless goodness. In the *Dialogue* of St Catherine of Siena, the eternal Father replies to the saint's question: "I will have mercy on the world, I will have mercy on the Church . . . for I have shown you that mercy is my distinctive property."'[8] 'And no one can say, "this is worse than that", for all things shall prove good in their season' (Sir 39:34).

'All shall be well': this is the key phrase which throws light on the problem of evil. The angel sees the outcome, which provides an explanation for all the difficulties and all the pain; man, limited to the light of reason, does not know the outcome and he rebels against suffering; a believer whose faith is weak bears suffering with a bad grace, whereas the Christian who has a strong faith believes in this happy outcome. And the more firmly he believes, in the dark of his night, the greater share he has (though he never has as much as they) in the imperturbable serenity which angels have in the face of evil; this serenity is strengthened by the effects of his acts of faith on his intelligence, his will and his feelings. A deep sense of peace is one of the characteristics of God's friends.

It is there in the depth of their soul and it flows right up into their face and eyes.

Perfect harmony

There is another feature of the holiness of the guardian angels which impressed St Thomas Aquinas and various founders of religious institutes like Ignatius Loyola, Vincent de Paul, John Baptist de la Salle, Francis Libermann and Mary Theresa Soubiran—the perfect way they combine active and contemplative life.

Christ himself points to this harmony when he says that the angels of children continuously see the face of his Father: they contemplate God and at the same time they are acting as guardians of men. What the Archangel Gabriel says to Zechariah also displays this harmony: 'I am Gabriel, who *stands in the presence* of God; and I was sent to speak to you, and to bring you this good news' (Lk 1:19). Without leaving God's presence for a single moment, Gabriel fulfils his mission in Judea. For him adoration of God and mission to men are one and the same thing. These two activities fuse together.

His intervention in the life of his protégé on earth in no way prevents an angel from contemplating unceasingly the face of God in heaven: it is a case of being 'contemplative in action' and 'active in contemplation'.

So, whereas one finds in many apostles, clerical and lay, a lamentable cleavage between their external activities and their interior life, the contrary happens in the case of angels: external activities and interior life are fused. They have no problem of achieving continuity, there is no split of any kind. Contemplation and action form in them that magnificent symbiosis which is proposed as an ideal by the masters of the spiritual life and which Vatican II has reminded us of. For angels contemplation of God is 'topped out' by their fulfilling their role in God's government of the world and by cooperating with God in the redemption of men.

What is the secret of this synthesis? For the guardian angel, St Thomas Aquinas explains, intervening in the daily lives of men means putting into practice the thoughts and designs which he contemplates in God. Just as the sculptor in working on a block of marble gives external expression to the idea in his mind, so the angel, when he prevents a person from taking a wrong step, by enlightening him, reminding him of some forgotten resolution, carries out in the world the plans he contemplates in God.

There is a continuity running right through, from angels' contemplation in heaven to their particular work on earth, the sort of continuity that obtains between a plan and its execution. Contemplation of God and his designs is what regenerates the work of angels in the service of men.

St Thomas brings his analysis further still: there is nothing in the external activity of the angels which is not connected with contemplation of God, the source of their blessedness. 'Just as an artist thinks carefully about the work he plans to execute, the angel at one and the same time contemplates God and renders service to men.'[9]

The service of men does not mean that angels interrupt their principal activity; it is not a secondary role for them, a sort of pastime or, worse still, a chore, as looking after children can be a nuisance for certain parents of intellectual or artistic temperament. The service of men is part of the essential activity of guardian angels and is the source of their unalloyed happiness.

However, our everyday experience does suggest an objection to this idea of fusion of contemplation and action in angels. St Thomas is on record as saying that external occupations are an obstacle to contemplation of the truth. And in sacred Scripture we read: 'He who has little business may become wise' (Sir 38:24).

A person who spreads himself too thinly is not well equipped for intellectual work. If a teacher of philosophy gets very involved in sport or gardening or hobbies he has to eat into the time and energy his real work calls for.

This is the way the saint solves this difficulty. In the case of men 'external tasks do hinder the purity of contemplation, since we engage in activity by means of the sense powers whose functionings, when they are intense, retard the activities of the intellect. Angels, however, direct their external actions by means of pure intellectual activity so that their external acts do not hinder their contemplation at all; for in the case of two activities, one of which is the rule and rationale of the other, the former does not hinder the latter but rather aids it.' Therefore St Gregory says[10] that 'the angels do not go abroad in such a way that they lose the delights of inner contemplation'.[11]

Cleavage between interior life and external activity is a great temptation for an apostle, particularly so in our own time, which tends to lay too much stress on man's abilities and to underestimate the effects of original sin. This leads to the risk of applying to apostolate methods which are valid for commercial advertizing and political propaganda—whereas the whole history of the Church bears witness to the truth of these words of Christ himself about the key to fruitful apostolate: 'He who abides in me, and I in him, he it is that bears much fruit' (Jn 15:5).

'*Abiding in Christ*' is not just a matter of visiting him at different times during the day: Mass, divine office, meditation, spiritual reading or some other practice of piety. '*Abiding in Christ*' is being with him all the time through faith, hope and charity, and being constantly inspired by his Spirit.[12] The guardian angels are perfect models of this: they abide in God even while they are visiting our world. 'The angels are always in God, and . . . God acts always in them in a free and full manner.'[13]

Unity and faithfulness

A mystic to whom we have already referred, Lucie-Christine, shows us the advantages of this continuity between interior life and external activity, which is to be found in a perfect form in angels and more or less imperfectly in apostles, whether priests or laypeople. She also points out the bad effects—even the bad effects on one's health—of apostolic activity which is disconnected from contemplation of God and, therefore, is deprived of inner unity.

It is desirable that 'in all things self-love be replaced by the desire for the love and glory of God . . . The soul is wearied, not so much by its activity as by the passion and self-interest with which it acts (be that action interior or exterior). The more it is "caught up" in activities, the more passion and self-interest tire and weary us, as our intention keeps changing from one thing to the next. Right intention, by contrast, means single-mindedness, a single purpose in everything: the soul finds rest in its activity and also the source of greater truthfulness. . . . This is the secret of the amazing achievements of the saints.'[14] This multiplicity of motives is precisely what we do not find in the guardian angels: they have only one reason for acting—the will of God.

Another contemporary French mystic, Marie-Antoinette de Geuser, endowed with exceptional graces, seems to have experienced to a rare degree this happy marriage of interior conversation with God and external conversation with others. She flows freely from one to the other. Love of God nourishes her love for her neighbour and vice versa. 'The more I give myself to external duties, the more aware am I of Jesus, the more I listen to him.'[15]

'There was a time . . . when I was unable to give myself completely to God and to other people at the same time . . . Now I can keep up two conversations almost effortlessly . . . , or, better, it is all the one thing . . .'[16] 'Since I see only God in everything and in everyone, how could his will be an obstacle for our union?'[17]

In the case of Christians, this synthesis of internal life and service of men depends on a genuine life of faith. Pius XII puts it this way, when addressing some nursing sisters, 'If you have a living faith, if behind those human faces—faces twisted by pain or wasted by illness; faces burning with fever; faces restless in the thought that their illness is getting worse; impassive, resigned faces—if behind those faces you are able to discover Jesus everywhere in the hospital, lying in every bed, motionless in the mysterious solemnity of the operating theatres, you will not even realize that you have moved from the chapel to the wards; you will not be concerned about any danger that your religious observance might get in the way of your attention to the sick, or vice versa. You will continue loving him under whatever form and wherever he is to be found. There will be no interruption in your conversation with him, no obstruction, no forgetting what he is and what he wishes.'[18]

He is never more active . . .
'No interruption in our conversation' with God, even when engaged in the most absorbing external activity—this is the ideal St Ignatius spoke of when he confided to Fr Ribadeneira his desire 'to be like the angels, who are not distracted by any of their occupations, who never cease to see God and to enjoy him'.

We can understand, then, why despite the profound difference between the spiritual nature of an angel and the matter-plus-soul nature of man, so many founders of modern religious orders and congregations have 'proposed to their sons and daughters that they take as their model the pure spirits in heaven. In the Church the expression *bios angelicos*, angelic life, is still used to designate the monastic state; and Pius XII wrote that the vocation of those who consecrate themselves entirely to God is an 'angelic vocation'.[19]

The Church herself, in her liturgy, recommends to all the faithful that they imitate the angels.[20]

'*Ecce somniator venit!*' Joseph's brothers exclaim when they see him coming: 'Here comes the dreamer.' So-called modern, up-to-date Christians may dismiss as dreams the views of an Ignatius Loyola or a Vincent de Paul about the guardian angels. Yet history is there to prove that mysticism has given the Church her greatest men of action.[21]

'Action and contemplation become one; they fuse together. To abide in God, the soul must obey the motion of the Holy Spirit, who takes her here and there to do his work. Wherever she is brought, there she finds God, who brings her to himself in the sweet clarity of the experience of her soul. She is never more active, never stronger, than when God installs her in the solitude of contemplation; she is never more united to God, never more contemplative, than when she gives herself to works in order to do the will of God and under the influence of the Holy Spirit.'[22]

It can truly be said that a soul like that is imitating the angels. Because they continuously see the Invisible One and are joined to him with their entire being, angels act effectively upon the visible world. They share in the irresistible power of God.

Holy Scripture says of Moses, a man of action and of prayer, that he acted with as much assurance 'as if he had seen him who is invisible' (Heb 11:27).

Sitting at his gate

Some time ago I showed the late Cardinal Journet some reflections on the part played by angels in everyday life. 'Yes,' he replied, 'yes, the angels do show themselves, but to those who love them and invoke them.'

'Have confidence in your guardian angel', Blessed J. Escrivá writes. 'Treat him as a lifelong friend—that is what he is—and he will render you a thousand services in ordinary affairs each day.'[1]

The connection between invocation of angels and being helped by them is clearly to be seen from the Bible, the writings of the doctors and the experience of the saints. 'Our needs rise on wings of prayer, and God's help comes down to us on wings of angels.'

When wretchedness cries out, mercy cannot but reply.

We use the word 'prayer' here in its broadest sense—the raising of the soul to God. This happens not only through the prayer of petition, adoration, expiation and thanksgiving, but also through an upright life, a life attentive to God and directed towards him. 'Man prays whenever he directs all his activity to God,' St Thomas says, commenting on the parable about the need always to pray and not lose heart (Lk 18:1)[2]

Because of his faith, Abraham merits being visited by three mysterious travellers who announce to him the birth of Isaac. Because of the purity of his life in the midst of a corrupt society, Lot, his wife and his daughters merit being saved from the terrible punishment inflicted on the inhabitants of Sodom.

The Book of Tobias starts with the double drama of an old man afflicted with blindness and the despair of a young woman who has buried seven husbands, one after the other. Tobias and Sarah, in their desolation, raised their prayers to heaven. 'The prayer of both was heard in the presence of the glory of the great God. And Raphael was sent to heal the two of them' (Tob 3:16). The gall of the fish caught by the younger Tobias restored the old man's sight and Sarah was released from the evil demon Asmodeus.

'If you hearken to his voice . . .'
The instructions which God gives the chosen people, listed in
Exodus 23, also show the causal link between prayer and angel's
help. The liturgy uses this text as a reading on the feast of the
guardian angels. In its literal sense it is an exhortation to obey the
angel charged with leading the Israelites out of the desert into the
Promised Land. In its figurative sense, which is the sense used in
the missal, it invites the faithful to follow the inspirations of the
guardian angels charged with leading them through the dangers
of life on earth into the promised land of heaven. To this is added
the promise of the almighty help of God himself. 'I shall send an
angel before you, to guard you on the way and to bring you to the
place which I have prepared. Give heed to him and hearken to his
voice, do not rebel against him, for he will not pardon your
transgression; for my name is in him.' There follow, in metaphori-
cal words, the promises God links to docility towards his angel: 'If
you hearken attentively to his voice and do all that I say, then I will
be an enemy to your enemies and an adversary to your adversary;
and my angel will go before you' (Ex 23:20-23).

People who are attentive and docile to the inspirations of the
angel, who make God's will known, will have God as an ally. He
himself will defend their cause. In a few striking verses Psalm 34
gives a dramatic sketch—the prayer of an unfortunate man, freedom at the hand of an angel, joy, an invitation to confidence. 'This
poor man cried, and the Lord heard him, and saved him out of all
his troubles. The angel of the Lord encamps around those who fear
him, and delivers them. Taste and see that the Lord is good! Happy
is the man who takes refuge in him' (Ps 34:7-9). To show the prayer
of the guardian angel, who shares in God's omnipotence, the
inspired author uses the image of trench warfare.

Psalm 91 sings of the protective power of God and shows the
multiple ways in which God acts to save his own. In particular it
emphasizes the role of angels. Here, as in other passages of Scripture, Providence intervenes in response to an act of abandonment,
such as that at the start of the psalm: 'My refuge and my fortress;
my God, in whom I trust.'

In spite of being a pagan, King Nebuchadnezzar nobly recognizes that it was fidelity to the true God that miraculously saved
the three young Hebrews thrown into the fiery furnace: 'Blessed
by the God of Shadrach, Meshach and Abednego, who has sent his
angel and delivered his servants, who trusted in him, and set at

naught the king's command, and yielded up their bodies rather than serve and worship any god except their own God' (Dan 3:28).

'I have come because of your words'
This cause and effect relationship is also confirmed by an angel who appears to Daniel. Daniel trembles with fear and prostrates himself on the ground: 'O Daniel, . . . stand upright, for know I have been sent to you . . . Fear not, for from the first day that you set your mind to understand and humbled yourself before your God, your words have been heard, and I have come because of your words' (Dan 10:1-12). Daniel's prayer ascends, the angel descends.

Prayer also causes the dramatic intervention by angels which we read of in the Book of the Maccabees. The entire people set to prayer when Heliodorus broke into the temple to take its treasure. 'When the army of Timothy was approaching, Maccabeus and his men sprinkled dust upon their heads and girded their loins with sackcloth, in supplication to God' (2 Mac 10:25).

The evangelists tell us of two visits by angels to Christ: one when he was at the end of his forty-day fast in the desert; the other during his agony in the garden of Gethsemani. On both occasions it is while he is praying that the angels visit the 'Son of Man'.

While he is serving as a priest in the temple, Zechariah is visited by an angel, who announces the birth of the Precursor. And tradition shows Mary at prayer when the Archangel Gabriel appears and reveals to her the mystery of the Incarnation.

After a first arrest and first release of the apostles (Acts 5:17-20), Herod once more arrests Peter and leaves him in the custody of four squads of soldiers. 'So Peter was kept in prison; but earnest prayer for him was made to God by the Church' (Acts 12:4-5). The night before he was due to appear for trial, Peter was rescued in a spectacular way. 'Peter was sleeping between two soldiers, bound with two chains, and sentries before the door were guarding the prison; and behold, an angel of the Lord appeared, and a light shone in the cell; and he struck Peter on the side and woke him saying, "Get up quickly." And the chains fell off his hands. And the angel said to him, "Dress yourself and put on your sandals." And he did so. And he said to him, "Wrap your mantle around you and follow me." And he went out and followed him; he did not know that what was done by the angel was real, but thought he was seeing a vision. When they had passed the first and second guard, they came to the iron gate leading into the city. It opened to them of its own accord, and they went out and passed on through one street; and immediately the angel left him. And Peter came to himself and said, "Now I am sure that the Lord has sent his angel and rescued me from the hand of Herod and from all that the Jewish people were expecting" ' (Acts 12:6-11).

The Acts also report two appearances of angels to St Paul during his apostolic journeys. In the middle of a great storm, when his boat was about to sink, he received unexpected encouragement: 'This very night there stood by me an angel of the God to whom I belong and whom I worship, and he said to me, "Do not be afraid, Paul; you must stand before Caesar; and lo, God has granted you all those who sail with you." So take heart, men' (Acts 27:23-25).

After traversing Asia Minor, Paul and his companions came to Troas, near the Dardanelles. 'And a vision appeared to Paul in the night: a man of Macedonia was standing beseeching him and saying, "Come over to Macedonia and help us." And when he had seen the vision, immediately we sought to go into Macedonia, concluding that God had called us to preach the gospel to them' (Acts 16:9-10). Through the intermediacy of an angel, under the appearance of a Macedonian, God at this point in history directed the apostolate of St Paul towards Europe.

They merit an angel's help
And it is another angel who brings about a meeting between the apostle Peter and a gentile 'who prayed constantly to God'. 'At Caesarea there was a man named Cornelius, a centurion of what was known as the Italian Cohort, a devout man who feared God with all his household, gave alms liberally to the people, and prayed constantly to God. About the ninth hour of the day he saw clearly in a vision an angel of God coming in and saying to him, "Cornelius". And he stared up at him in terror, and said "What is it, Lord?" And he said to him, "Your prayers and your alms have ascended as a memorial before God."' The angel went on to tell this gentile to send men to Joppa to get Simon called Peter. Also instructed in a vision Peter went to Cornelius' house and baptized him and his family (Acts 10:14).

Around the same time an angel spoke to Philip the deacon and told him to go out at noon to the road that went down from Jerusalem to Gaza. There, sitting in his chariot, was a minister of the queen of Ethiopia, returning from a pilgrimage to Jerusalem, and he was reading the prophet Isaiah. 'Do you understand what you are reading?' Philip asked him, prompted by the Holy Spirit. 'How can I, unless someone guides me?' the official replied. And he invited him to sit beside him. The deacon enlightened this noble soul who was seeking the light and when they reached a place where there was water, Philip baptized the Ethiopian (Acts 8:27).

The doctors of the Church and spiritual writers draw certain lessons from these coincidences between prayer (even prayer understood in a broad sense) and visits by angels.

St Thomas points out, in connection with the episode at the end of Jesus' fast in the desert, that those who resist devils merit the help of angels.[3] Resisting the devil's temptations is a logical result of being attached to the will of God. A person who says Yes to God, says No to God's foremost adversary. Someone who shuts out the devil, opens the door to God. People who open themselves to God, open themselves to his envoys on earth.

'It is said in St Luke that Christ, entering upon his agony, prayed at greater length, and that then an angel appeared to comfort him. All this happened for our sake,' St Bonaventure observes. 'Christ had no need of being borne up in this way: it was to show that the angels give much assistance to those who pray devoutly, that they support them and comfort them and that they also present their prayers to God.'[4]

To let the sun in

The less the soul is controlled by the senses, St Thomas observes, the more open is it to angels' inspirations.[5] This is why children and saints seem to be angels' favourites: natural innocence and purity achieved through real effort predispose people to receive enlightenment. 'No evil shall befall you, no scourge come near your tent,' Psalm 91, the hymn to the guardian angels, puts it. 'Consider that this promise is not made to men who live according to the flesh,' St Bernard comments, 'but to those who, though they are living in the flesh, are led by the spirit.'[6] 'How miserable we are,' the same saint exclaims, 'if our sins render us unworthy to receive the visit of the angels and enjoy their presence. If we have great need of the company of angels, we should carefully avoid offending them and should exercise ourselves in the practice of virtues which we know are pleasing to them, such as purity, voluntary poverty, fraternal correction.[7]

MY ANGEL

Blessed Peter Faber also points out that vice, and particularly over-eating or over-drinking, shuts a person off from the inspirations of the good angels and leaves them open to the influence of the bad angels. This is why he determined to 'be very moderate in eating and drinking and in all his external activity . . . realizing that it is very important that evil spirits should lose their ability to dwell in his body and influence his soul, for they cannot find there a heart besotted by food and drink.'[8]

What these spiritual writers are saying is nothing but the application of a general law which applies to both the natural level and the sphere of grace: in order to take on a new shape the material in question must have a certain predisposition for it. For the sun to brighten and warm a room the curtains have to be open. For liquid to fill a glass, the glass must be empty. For grace to impregnate a free creature, that creature has to be receptive. Grace never forces its way in. God respects the free action of the faculties which he himself has established.

To sum all this up in a few words, we might say that there are two agents at work—God's immeasurable love, which burns to spread itself, and man's profound need, of which often he is unaware.

'A nothing surrounded by God'

'God desires only one thing in this world, the only thing he needs, but he desires it so strongly that he devotes himself entirely to it. This is that one thing—to find empty and ready that basic nobility he himself has placed in man's noble spirit, so that there he can bring to perfection his noble and divine work. God has all the power in heaven and on earth; but just one thing is lacking to him—not being able to accomplish in man the most exquisite of all his works'. This is the human language Tauler[9] uses to express the desire which consumes God to give, to give uninterruptedly, to give without measure provided man is receptive to him.

'Man', says Cardinal de Bérulle, 'is a nothing surrounded by God, in need of God, with a capacity for God, who can be full of God if he so wishes.'[10]

Countless passages of Holy Scripture show the intimate connection that exists between this openness on man's part and the outpouring of grace.

'Beloved, I stand at the door and knock; if any one hears my voice and opens the door, I will come in to him and eat with him, and he with me' (Rev 3:20).

'She [Wisdom] is easily discerned by those who love her, and is found by those who seek her. She hastens to make herself known to those who desire her. He who rises early to seek her will have no difficulty, for he will find her sitting at his gates' (Wis 6:13-15).

The Almighty, Mary proclaims, 'has filled the hungry with good things, and the rich he has sent empty away' (Lk 1:53).

Everyone is poor, but not everyone recognizes his need. Prayer helps people discover their neediness. Prayer tells God nothing, because he knows our needs even before we are born. Nor is it the purpose of prayer to press God in the strict sense of the word, and to get him to give us today what he seemed to deny us yesterday. God does not change his mind. What prayer does is undermine man's pride which blocks off grace just as a shutter prevents the light from entering a room.[11]

The doctors of the Church are for ever emphasizing this. In their analysis of unhealthy passions and their effects on men's behaviour, a Thomas Aquinas or a John of the Cross points out the extent to which the outpouring of grace is conditioned by men's moral dispositions.

Does this mean that the Almighty is powerless in the face of our evil dispositions, that we can erect an insurmountable obstacle to grace? No. St Thomas says that God in his omnipotence can create the right dispositions in people. If these dispositions are there already, he avails of them and that is the normal way grace operates; if they are missing, he can certainly cause them but that is exceptional—as in the cases of dramatic conversions, where there is no human explanation.[12] For 'God who is universal cause in the order of action does not antecedently require, in corporeal effects, either matter or any material predisposition. God can immediately cause to be, all at once, matter, disposition and form' (St Thomas).[13]

The principle given by the Angelic Doctor has general application. If the entry of grace is normally conditioned by the presence of good dispositions, God in his omnipotence can, as an exception, just because he chooses to do so, create these dispositions.

These considerations about the conditions in which grace in general and angels in particular operate, contain the answer to one of the objections that may be posed: why are there so many sins around? Why not enlighten sinners? The answer is simple: it is not enough for the guardian angel to give a person good inspirations: these inspirations need to be well received.

These considerations also throw light on another aspect of the angels' mission: the special favour people enjoy who keep up a friendly relationship with them. These favours should not surprise us. They may seem to be more than men deserve, but they are well within the scope of God's love: we will never be able to understand God's thirst to give himself, to pour himself into our hearts.[14]

If on a cloudless day a room is filled with light, this is because the rays of the sun have been able to get in. If the room were in darkness the fault would lie with whoever failed to open the curtains.

The angels are rays of light shining from God: 'they do show themselves, but only to those who love them and invoke them.'

Looking to the future

'The time is coming when people will not endure sound teaching, but having itching ears they will accumulate for themselves teachers to suit their own likings.' And in their desire to hear new things 'they will turn away from listening to the truth and wander into myths' (2 Tim 4:3-4).

The Church often reminds the faithful of this warning against walking away from sound teaching and looking for new things: this text occurs in one of the readings in the Mass of doctors of the Church.

The doctrinal confusion which is a feature of our own time should make us think about what the Apostle says. These days, Paul VI has pointed out, every truth is questioned. The German philosopher Dietrich von Hildebrand denounces the appearance of *The Trojan horse in the City of God.* Jacques Maritain saw this 'kind of *kneeling before the world* as one of the strangest features of the current crisis of Catholicism.[1] Fr Louis Bouyer analyses the 'decomposition' of Catholicism. Hans Urs von Balthasar finishes his book *Cordula* with a chapter entitled 'When the salt loses its savour'. It consists of a dialogue between a political commissar and a Christian suffering from the disease of kneeling before the world: 'Your Christianity is not worth a round of ammunition; you have liquidated yourselves: it saves us the bother of persecuting you.'

'The Church', Paul VI said, 'is in a period of restlessness, of self-criticism, even, one might say, of self-destruction. It is a kind of complex, acute, internal revolution, which no one would have expected to follow the Council.'[2]

'You have liquidated yourselves', 'a period of . . . self-destruction'—the same idea, coming from different sources.

St Paul's warning, which the liturgy makes its own, could also be applied to what is happening to the Church's teaching on the role of angels. On the one hand, we have Paul VI in the *Creed of the people of God* affirming the role of angels, and Pius XI, Pius XII and John XXIII encouraging the faithful to be on familiar terms with

MY ANGEL

the angels; on the other, angels are being attacked: the guardian angels are undergoing a process of demystification.'[3]

Is this attack on angels not an additional reason for the faithful to hold on to the teaching of the Church? If God allows revealed truths to be questioned, does this not give believers an opportunity to go deeper into Church doctrine, to get a better grasp of its basics and clear away any excrescence? By causing healthy reactions of this sort, the people who are attacking the theology of angels could well become, despite themselves its best promoters.

Decline and development

For some years now, more and more has been written about angels. There have been theological conferences on angels—for example in Germany and France.[4] The editor of a French journal of spirituality told me that the only article in the course of the year that had provoked lots of grateful letters from readers was one on the role of the guardian angels in everyday life in the light of Scripture and Tradition. The author, a layman, was not a professional theologian, unlike most of the contributors to the journal. Many Christians are interested in the angels.

The contemporary development of angelology brings to mind an idea of St John of the Cross: the more people's miseries increase, the more God multiplies his mercies. In order to counteract the influence of naturalism in the world, Providence led the supreme Magisterium of the Church to proclaim the dogmas of the Immaculate Conception (1854) and the Assumption of our Lady (1950). These definitions led to a renewal of Marian piety and mariology.

The same thing may well happen in regard to angels. The Holy Spirit, the soul of the Church, can show us more clearly the full implications of certain phrases in the Bible which we have tended to miss. As Paul VI put it: 'All that is needed is to pay a little more attention to discover that apparently modest expressions are full of vigour, rich in content, widely applicable, theologically and humanly deep, containing a Truth which really expresses itself in all its essence, which is divine.'[5] Thanks to the dogma of the Immaculate Conception we now know much better the deep meaning of the Archangel Gabriel's greeting to Mary: 'Full of grace'. Perhaps a day will come when Christians will realize more clearly than we do the practical applications of the promise 'He will give his angels charge over you to guard you in all your ways' (Ps 91:11).

A friendly presence when we are alone

Devotion to the angels would seem to be particularly suitable for dealing with one difficulty which is very common nowadays—the feeling of loneliness and insecurity.

If it is true that Christian faith grows when it is practiced in elites, it is also true that it diminishes in huge masses. The number of committed Christians seems to go down. On the other hand, minority groups of Christians can feel isolated and threatened and this drains them of energy. People can feel isolated even in the context of Christian homes and religious communities: 'I feel as if I am on my own . . . I have no support . . . I have to swim against the current . . .'[6] An attitude of bowing down before the world prevents people from asserting themselves spiritually. Not to mention those men and women who over the years live alone in their fidelity to God, without the encouragement of friends, the stimulus of meeting supportive people. . . .

But think of the light and support and joy these men and women would have if they *realized* the continuous presence of their angel at their side. It is not a matter of their becoming intellectually aware of angels, as happens when someone listens to a theoretical paper on angels: it is a vivid, concrete awareness, the sort of awareness you have when you are deep in conversation with a very close friend.

Monsignor Jean Calvet, when he was dean of the faculty of arts at the Institut Catholique in Paris, told of how he was reminded of the existence of the guardian angels by the example of a farmworker. 'I was taking a walk down a shady country road when I came across an old lady. She was very bent-over and using a stick.

"Good day to you, Catinelle."

She half straightened up and replied, "And to you, father and your company."

"How's that? I am on my own; where's my company?"

She straightened up completely; I could see her heavily lined face, and her eyes, still beautiful. She said to me, very seriously, "And your angel guardian, where did you leave him?"

"Thank you, gran. I was forgetting my guardian angel. Thanks for reminding me." '

This little episode led Monsignor Calvet to thinking and praying much more about the angels: 'I have arranged a little corner in my oratory for my guardian angel.'[7]

Caesare Angelini has written some very moving pages about

the angels. He tells us how he was present at Compline in a very old abbey and felt very moved by the words of the prayer the Abbot said. The Abbot spoke with great conviction: 'Come to this hearth, Lord . . . May your angels dwell here and keep us at peace.'

Angelini went back to his cell. As soon as he closed the door he felt absolutely certain he was not alone. He noticed a mysterious presence. He felt that an angel was there, for him, for him alone. The writer was then filled with a deep joy, such as he had never experienced before.

'Faith is the act of believing in what one doesn't see,' says St Augustine, and Newman defines the Christian as a man who believes what he does not see.

That is the position of Christians who believe unreservedly in the presence of their guardian angels: the invisible is for them something real, something almost visible.

Like X-rays

To understand what this certainty means and not relegate it to the category of a dream or autosuggestion, let us refer to a truth of religious psychology, with the help of St Thomas: supernatural forces, which derive from God, are more powerful than natural energies, which depend on human nature. Through faith, men share in the knowledge which God has of himself and of creation. Through faith, men in some way see their guardian angel through God's eyes. Through faith, the Christian discerns a presence where his spirit, if it uses only its natural resources, can see nothing at all.

This insight which faith gives can be compared with X-rays. Whereas sunlight and electric light can expose only the surface of a patient's body, X-rays go through and reach his bone-structure. The bone-structure is there, even though natural light and electric light do not show it. Similarly, angels really do exist, even if the cameraman's flash, psychologists' texts, sociologists' surveys and journalists' reports cannot cover them.

To discover some things special instruments are needed. Some stars are visible only through a telescope. Can we deny that they exist because the man in the street cannot see them simply by looking up?

Let us go back to one episode in Holy Scripture which shows how faith makes us see further. It takes place in Dothan, where the prophet Elisha and his servant Gehazi live. The king of Syria has surrounded the city by night. 'When the servant of the man of God rose early in the morning and went out, behold, an army with horses and chariots was round about the city. And the servant said, "Alas, my master! What shall we do?" He said, "Fear not, for those who are with us are more than those who are with them."'

It was faith which led Elisha to realize this superiority. Gehazi, who had less faith, did not see it. The servant needed more light from on high. 'Elisha prayed, and said, "O Lord, I pray thee, open his eyes that he may see." So the Lord opened the eyes of the young man, and he saw; and behold, the mountain was full of horses and chariots of fire round about Elisha' (2 Kg 6:14-19). This heavenly army was a revelation of the power of angels.

Lucie-Christine, whose intense faith led her to believe in angels as if she were seeing them with her very eyes, thought that if we could continually see the angels who surround us and protect us, we would lose any sense of our own disabilities and evils, but this would not be good for us on earth.[8]

In other words, we would see that those evil forces which make us uneasy or even worry us, whether in our daily lives or in the sphere of international politics or in the life of the Church are, to tell the truth, under the control of Providence; Providence uses the forces of evil to purify God's friends, just as a dentist uses a drill to remove decay from a tooth. Never at any point in history does God lose absolute control of events. Always, even in the darkest periods of the history of the Church and the life of nations, the faithful angels have the edge on the rebellious angels. The least of the good angels rules over Lucifer himself, the prince of the rebellious angels, and elicits his obedience, St Thomas says.[9]

This supremacy is based on the fact that the will of the good angel is completely attached to God's plans, plans which are implemented infallibly, always and everywhere. 'Every man or angel, in so far as he is united to God, becomes one spirit with God, and is thus superior to every other creature.'[10]

Joan of Arc's splendid reply to the Bastard of Orleans throws light on this tactical superiority of leaders who adhere to the plans of God. 'In the name of God, the counsel of Messire (that is, God) is better than yours and better than that of men; and it is sounder and wiser. You have sought to deceive me, but you have deceived yourselves. For I bring you a better aid than any knight, town or city has ever had. And it is God's good pleasure and the support of the King of the Heavens, sent not out of consideration for me

104

but straight from God, who through the prayers of St Louis and St Charlemagne has taken pity on the city of Orleans.'[11]

Familiarity with the angels gives a sense of security. Our invisible companions communicate to us something of that peace they desire from God, who is truly 'the Lord of history' (Pius XII).

The desert blooms

However, if we saw the angels only as protectors we would be seeing only one aspect of their mission. If a city needs a police force and an army, it also needs teachers, writers and artists. The angel guardian not only acts as a barrier or dyke or wall; he is also a medium, a source of encouragement, a light. He has a mission not only of keeping physical and moral evil away from us, but also, and especially, of leading us towards good. Like a mountain guide, the angel goes ahead of his protégé: 'Behold, I send an angel before you, to guard you on the way and to bring you to the place which I have prepared . . . My angel will go before you' (Ex 23:20, 23).

People who open themselves to his inspirations and his radiation experience this presence of light and love. Their fellow traveller gives them encouragement and joy such as they will never find among men. 'Only those souls who let themselves be guided by their angels, who have a friendly relationship with them, who love them, who honour them and confidently invoke them, can speak of the power and goodness and generous refinement of these divine sowers of perfection.'[12]

But there is a difference between angels' friendship and that of men. 'The guardian angels never abandon us, though we may abandon God', St Francis de Sales says. The angel's love for man is lucid, pure, strong and constant; it is not subject to ups and downs; it is not careless, forgetful or unfaithful. The angel's love derives from God's love for men; and it is from this love that he gets his constancy and sovereign disinterestedness. Human beings' love for each other is something different. So many things can influence it: a headache makes us irritable, an ambiguous remark makes us touchy, an offence causes resentment. We all have experience of how misunderstanding or differences of opinions can undermine warm friendships, how clashes of personality can occur within families or religious communities.

None of these faults are to be found in guardian angels. Whether someone responds to their friendship or not, they continue to do their job. They stay faithful to their mission even if a person is unfaithful to his duties to them. They keep holding his hand even if he turns his back on them or closes his ears to their inspirations. 'My angel thinks about me, but I never think about him,' she confessed, confused, after reading a study on angels. '"Roderick, I am yours! Roderick, I'm coming",' exclaims one of Paul Claudel's heroines, on the edge of perdition. 'I am going with you,' her guardian angel declares.[13]

In some countries there is a telephone service where you can 'dial a friend', which is designed to help lonely people. 'I feel useless, I am lonely. The nights are terrible.' 'I go to the pictures and I spend the time asking myself: What will I do later? I'll go for a walk. And after that?' Would someone in this position not be amazed if they were told they had an angel constantly at their side who sees them and loves them and burns with desire to fill their solitude and make their desert bloom, leading them to use their time and energy in the service of God and of men?

We can never insist enough on the harmony that exists between the initiative God and the angels take, and the hidden hopes that abide in a person's heart and soul. God is love. Jesus came on earth 'to seek and save the lost' (Lk 19:10). Like water, grace seeks out a space in order to fill it. Like the sun, God's gifts look for spaces to fill with light. The guardian angels second these operations. They are true friends to us. An underdeveloped notion of the Mystical Body leads us to undervalue this friendship.

Paul VI pointed this out when canonizing that friend of the angels, Brother Benildus of the Brothers of the Christian Schools: he strove to strengthen people's sense of the communion of saints: awareness of the fact, as St Paul puts it, that we are 'fellow citizens with the saints and members of the household of God' (Eph 2:9).[14]

'It might be said,' Jacques Maritain wrote, 'that we stupidly believe that this people [the elect in heaven and the angels] sleep in the beatific vision and do not want to see anymore of us; they have forgotten about us. And furthermore it could be said that as far as we ourselves are concerned, we make it possible for this to happen.'[15] 'Both the angels and the saints in heaven', Dom Cipriano Vagaggini points out, 'are greatly interested in their brothers who are still involved in the struggle, and they help them in many ways: they offer God the prayers of the faithful; they pray to God for them of their own accord, constantly; the angels act as intermediaries between God and the faithful here below; they reveal God's plans to them; they take part in the battle as God's ministers,

MY ANGEL

to punish the enemies and followers of the beast, especially by means of material elements over which God has given them power; led by their prince, Michael, they also wage war directly on Satan and his minions.'[16]

'We live with angels'

'The hidden God, the mysterious God, is not the distant God, the absent God: he is always the God close to us.'[17] For 'in him we live and move and have our being'. Similarly, we might say that the hidden, mysterious angel is not distant or absent: he is always near us, like God, whose envoy is among men. He is with us all the time, wherever we go and he cooperates in every good thing we do. 'For here below we already live in the company of the angels,' St Thomas writes, out of his own experience of contemplation. When questioned about the presence of angels. Joan of Arc told her judges, 'I have seen them often among the Christians.'[18]

To explain to his parishioners how angels are always by our side, Newman recalled the angels whom Jacob saw in a dream, as ascending and descending. Jacob here is an image of man, who is continuously being looked after by the guardian angels, bringing as they do our prayers to heaven and heaven's lights and energies to us. 'Let this be observed. People commonly speak as if the other world did not exist now, but would after death. No: it exists now, though we see it not. It is among us and around us. Jacob was shown this in his dream. Angels were all about him' though he had not realized it. In other words, 'we are . . . in a world of spirits, as well as in a world of sense, and we hold communion with it, and take part in it, though we are not conscious of doing so.' Why, then, rebel against the mystery, whose existence our faith attests?[19]

Aware, like Newman, of the presence of the invisible world, Paul Claudel tries to analyze the mysterious way the guardian angel radiates on man: 'The pace with which we advance is at one and the same time ours and him.' By ourselves we would be incapable of this triumphal lightness, this modesty and, at the same time, this sureness. That little rhyme which I say now and then to cheer myself up—like the songs which I used to teach my children—I learned from his lips. It is he who cleansed my eyes with the ineffable gall of the fish. It is he who has made me see everything in a new way and who has placed under my feet the colour of blue sky which makes the most difficult road bearable.

It is he who extracts from everything for me morality and thanks-giving and who makes everything to the right and left of me turn into rhythm, idea, likeness, resolution, temperament and hymn. . . . Once this conversation between the pilgrim and his companion has begun, who can stop it? What a joy it is to hear him, and what a lot of things we should offer him?'[20]

More than that: once a person is familiar with his guardian angel he glimpses something of his mysterious beauty. 'I do not believe', a theolgian writes, 'that all the perfections, all the beauty in the world can compare with the perfection and beauty of an angel. St Thomas says somewhere that every angel is as brilliant as a star or a sun in the universe.'[21]

Angela of Foligno had the same feeling. When she was praying in the cathedral of Foligno she invoked the angels. They appeared to her: 'The presence of the angels filled me with joy: if I had not felt it I would not have believed that the sight of the angels could cause such joy.'[22]

A lay woman of our own time, canonized by Pius XII in 1940, St Gemma Galgani, enjoyed, like St Frances of Rome, the sight of her own guardian angel. She was on familiar terms with him. He was like an older brother to her, clear-minded, tender, sometimes severe and demanding: he did not let a fault go by without taking her to task. At first the saint's spiritual director doubted that she could actually see her angel. 'I noticed that every time she lifted her eyes to look at the angel, to listen to him or to speak to him, even if it were not while she was meditating or praying, she lost the use of her senses; at these times you could shake her or stick a pin in her and she would feel nothing. As soon as she looked away from her guardian angel or stopped talking to him, she became herself again . . . I say this in case people should say this intimate relationship with her angel was a hallucination.'[23]

The familiar relationship St Gemma Galgani had with her angel is undoubtedly exceptional—as exceptional as her life of prayer and penance in the middle of the world. Her spiritual director never ceases to point out that God distributes his graces according to each person's particular vocation. 'Hence it follows that the role of the guardian angel varies from person to person. Gemma was called by Providence to occupy a much higher place than is usual among the elect; this is why it was fitting that her angel should take such special care of her.'[24] Something Cardinal Danièlou says agrees with this: 'The greatest among the saints and men of God, from St Augustine to John Henry Newman, have always lived on familiar terms with (the angels)'.[25]

Hidden operators of the universe
I do not wish to finish these pages without mentioning one aspect which has not yet really been explored by authors—the relationship between angels and the universe at large. St Thomas throws some light on this relationship when he says, 'all material things are controlled by angels. This is the position not only of the doctors of the Church, but also of all the philosophers who postulate the existence of non-material beings.'[26]

'This, then, is a doctrine which is solidly established in tradition and in reason. With all due deference to the rationalism of certain of our contemporaries', Cardinal Danièlou comments, 'the intelligent and forceful government to which the order of the universe bears witness might very easily have heavenly spirits as its ministers. This bond between the angels and the visible universe, furthermore, could very well give us the key to certain mysteries.'[27]

'We might add that the discoveries of nuclear physics open up these horizons [of St Thomas] further, in a way we never before suspected,' Cardinal Journet writes. 'They let us into a world which is still the world of matter, yet where matter in some way shares the invisibility of spirit. Heisenberg's uncertainty principle shows us something which is still incomprehensible to us in this sphere. It is here that created pure spirits can act on the cosmos in a privileged and perhaps preponderant manner.'[28]

The relationship between angel and universe interested Newman very much. He saw the angels as operating the universe: 'I put it to any one, whether it is not as philosophical and as full of intellectual enjoyment, to refer the movements of the natural world to them, as it is to attempt to explain them by certain theories of science.'[29]

He criticizes man who 'curiously examines the works of Nature, as if they were lifeless and senseless; as if he alone had intelligence . . . Nature is not inanimate; its daily toil is intelligent; its works are duties . . . Thus, whenever we look abroad, we are reminded of the most gracious and holy Beings, the servants of the Holiest, who deign to minister to the heirs of salvation. Every breath of air and ray of light and heat, every beautiful prospect, is, as it were, the skirts of their garments, the waving of the robes of those whose faces see God in heaven . . .'

'Supposing the inquirer I have been describing, when examining a flower, or a herb, or a pebble, or a ray of light, which he treats as something so beneath him in the scale of existence, suddenly discovered that he was in the presence of some powerful being who was hidden behind the visible things he was inspecting, who though concealing his wise hand, was giving them their beauty, grace, and perfection, as being God's instrument for the purpose, say whose robe and ornaments those wondrous objects were, which he was so eager to analyse, what would be his thoughts? Should we but accidentally show a rudeness of manner towards our fellow-man, tread on the hem of his garment, or brush roughly against him, are we not vexed, not as if we had hurt him, but for fear that we may have been disrespectful? . . . how much has every herb and flower in it to surprise and overwhelm us! For, even did we know as much about them as the wisest of men, yet there are those around us, though unseen, to whom our greatest knowledge is as ignorance; and, when we converse on subjects of Nature scientifically, repeating the names of plants and earths, and describing their properties, we should do so religiously, as in the hearing of the great servants of God, with the sort of diffidence which we always feel when speaking before the learned and wise of our own mortal race . . . Now I can conceive persons saying all this is fanciful . . . Surely we are not told in Scripture about the Angels for nothing, but for practical purposes; nor can I conceive of a use of our knowledge more practical than to make it connect the sight of this world with the thought of another . . . Nor one more easily to be understood.'[30]

'But let us get this right', Fr Régamey very correctly argues. 'It is not a matter, in any sense, of including among those forces which modern physics is aware of, or may in the future discover, certain influences of a spiritual origin in such a way the material and spiritual combine to produce phenomena as we know them. We should not think that angelic influence can ever be grasped as such, in the way that physics has discovered protons, photons, cosmic rays, radar . . . We should not seek to find in the physical world a location for a spiritual action of this type: we are amazed to see excellent writers devote pages and pages to refuting this notion: two statements (which meet the demand for exactitutde which is an outstanding feature of modern science) sum it all up: (i) whatever is observed in the sphere of the sciences ought to be applied in that very same "field"; (ii) in this sphere one must consider scientifically non-existent whatever the senses cannot perceive by any experience as having its origin in observed reality.'[31]

Fr Régamey is here defining the area within which it is not *necessary* for the angels to intervene. Another theologian, Fr Lavy, also the author of a fine book on the angels, shows that their absolutely spiritual influence over the material world operates on a higher level. What Newman describes in the language of a poet and spiritual man, Fr Lavy expresses in the more rigorous language of the philosopher and theologian: 'The angels exercise a Providence even over the material world. It is difficult to explain this activity. We must avoid attributing to superior causes anything that can be adequately explained by natural causes. If science alone can explain the material world through the material world itself, there is no point in having recourse to superior causes; whereas, where nature cannot explain itself, it is reasonable to have recourse to superior agents.

'What nature cannot do is explain its own existence and that is what brings us to have recourse to a creative cause. Nature alone fails to explain its own movement, that motion which, pushing the world headlong into chaos yet brings it out of chaos. Movement in the universe as a whole has no explanation without a divine mover. "Movement", says Balzac, "breathes mysteriously from the sovereign maker of the worlds." This suggests there is room for a whole hierarchy of intermediaries. Notice that I am not removing from any lower cause, even from the elements, the action proper to them. St Thomas admits activity in bodies: "Material things have regular ways of behaviour deriving from the natures given to them by God" (*Summa Theologiae*, I, q. 110, a. 1). But, at the same time, he admits that they exercise this activity within a movement embedded in matter, a movement which does not derive from themselves. "Material things do exhibit regular behaviour, but they do so only in so far as they are acted upon since it is characteristic of material things not to act unless they are acted upon" (loc. cit., ad 1). It is in the womb of movement of whatever type (heat, light, electricity, etc) that everything takes shape in this world. I repeat, then, that angels can act in the movement of things but their action is higher action, about which physics can tell us nothing. "Angels change material things in a more perfect manner than do material agencies, in that, being the higher cause of the material agencies, they cause *them* to change" (loc. cit., a. 2 ad 2). St Augustine says that no movement occurs in space which does not presuppose a movement in time, nor does any movement in time occur which does not presuppose a vital movement, nor any vital movement without an intellectual movement.

'The obscurity surrounding this action, our difficulty in defining it, simply shows how much we don't know. For the deeper an action is the more hidden it is, just as God's action is the most hidden of all. In the case of physical agents themselves—light, heat, electricity—we can verify their action, but we do not know why they act, we do not even know their nature. Is it then surprising if we also fail to grasp what is going on in the case of the action of spirit on body, spirit on spirit, ultimately the action of God on all being?'[32]

These reflections of Cardinals Newman, Journet and Danièlou, and of Fathers Lavy and Régamey on the 'cosmic role' of angels illustrate what St Thomas says: through the ministry of angels God acts on the material world.

Angels seem to be, as it were, the long arm of the creator and his agents in the universe. But this whole area has still to be explored. Taken together, the researches of scientists, theologians and Christian philosophers can help to shed some light on it. 'The more one studies matter,' it has been wisely said, 'the more one discovers spirit in it'.[33] 'The more I find the presence of this spirit,' perhaps it will be said some day, 'the more I ask myself what is the source of that spirit and the channel through which that source communicates with the cosmos.'

That channel is the world of the angels.

To see the stars

Coming to the end of this book some readers may find themselves thinking about what the popes of our time have said about the angels and about their own experience—Pius XI's close relationship with his angel, how he used him to ease the way in difficult negotiations and how appreciative he was of his angel's help in all his good actions; Pius XII's invitation to live on familiar terms with those who will be our companions for eternity; John XXIII's desire to see a growth in devotion to the guardian angels; and Paul VI's reminder, in the *Creed of the People of God*, that the angels share in God's government of the universe.

These testimonies of the popes may seem surpising. They clash with the indifference towards angels which is frequently found. However, there is nothing sentimental or far-fetched about what the popes say. They are sober and reasonable. They describe things as they are. They open our eyes for us.

We could have spoken about 'the death of the angels', in the same language as 'the death of God'. In that connection Paul VI said that it is not that the sun has been put out, but that men's eyes have been darkened. God has not died in the way a great figure might die: he has died in the thoughts and in the hearts of many men and women.

'The death of the angels?' To draw a comparison: it is not that the stars have been put on; there are still myriads and myriads of stars, even if, in full daylight, man does not see them. To see the stars you must go into the darkness of the night. Similarly, to *see* the angels and converse with them, we need to penetrate the 'luminous darkness' of faith; we need to believe God: he himself has revealed their existence and the role they play in our lives.

Notes

INTRODUCTION
1. M. Bouttier, 'Angels' in *Vocabulaire biblique*, Neuchatel.
2. *De genesi ad litteram*, Book VIII, chap. 24, n. 45.
3. *Summa Theologiae*, I, q. 110, a. 1, ad 2.
4. Cf. Jacques Maritain, 'Le tenant-lieu de théologie chez les simples' in *Nova et Vetera*, 1969, no. 2, pp. 80-121.
5. Ibid., p. 104.
6. Ibid.
7. Ibid., p. 107.
8. *Sermo* 122, no. 5 (cf. *Sermo* 89, no. 5).

A DILEMMA
1. G.-M. Garrone, *This We Believe*, trs. M.A. Bouchard, Shannon 1969, p. 137.

I BELIEVE IN ANGELS
1. Address to Catholic children, 2 September 1934: *Discorsi di Pio XI*, vol. III, Turin 1960, pp. 196-200.
2. Address to Catholic explorers, 10 June 1923: *Discorsi di Pio XI*, vol. I, Turin 1959, p. 141.
3. Address of John XXIII in the Basilica of Our Lady of the Angels, Rome, 9 September 1962: *Discorsi, messagi, colloqui del Santo Padre Giovanni XXIII*, vol. IV, Vatican City 1959, p. 726.
4. Carlo Confalonieri, *Pio XI visto da vicino*, Turin 1957, pp. 308-309.
5. Cardinal Pellegrinetti, *Pio XI, l'uomo nel Papa, il Papa nell'uomo*, Rome 1939, p. 11.
6. Carlo Confalonieri, *op. cit.*, p. 309. In his book *Les merveilles divines opérées dans les ames par le ministère des anges* (Paris 1870, p. 366), Dom Benoit Sicard of the Trappist monastery at Sept-Fons, refers to how successful was St Peter Canisius' recourse to angels when he was on diplomatic missions: 'In the confessional, in the pulpit, on his journeys, on the various diplomatic missions he undertook on behalf of the Holy See, he always spoke to his guardian angel and confided in him; and in a life that lasted more than seventy two years he was successful in everything he did.'
7. AAS 1950, p. 570.
8. *Discorsi e radiomessagi di sua santità Pio XII*, vol. XX, pp. 413-414.
9. *Discorsi, messagi . . .Giovanni XXIII*, vol. III, Vatican City 1962, p. 450.
10. Apostolic exhortation, 6 January 1962: AAS 1962, p. 74.
11. Address, 30 September 1959: *Discorsi etc*, vol. I, p. 798.

12. Address, 24 October 1962: *Discorsi*, vol. IV, p. 860.

13. Address, 26 December 1962: *Discorsi*, vol. V, p. 328.

14. Jean Danièlou, *The Angels and their Mission*, trs. David Heimann, Westminster, Md. 1957 (reprinted 1982), p. viii.

15. Address, 9 August 1961: *Discorsi*, vol. III, p. 384.

16. Address, 12 December: *Discorsi*, vol. VI, p. 317.

17. John XXIII, *Lettres à ma famille*, Ed. du Cerf, 1969: letter, 3 October 1948.

18. Letter, 16 July 1968.

19. Cf. St Thomas, *Summa Theologiae*, I, q.113, a.1, ad 2.

20. *Summa Theologiae*, III, q.172, a.2.

21. In its statement on the *Dutch Catechism*, the commission of cardinals appointed by Paul VI in 1967 pointed clearly that the existence of angels is a truth of faith: 'The catechism must state that God has created, in addition to the physical world we live in, a kingdom of pure spirits which we call angels;' the cardinals referred to the Constitution *Dei Filius*, c. I of Vatican I and the Constitution *Lumen gentium*, nos. 49 and 50, of Vatican II. Previously, in a letter to Cardinal Alfrink, Primate of the Netherlands, among the material indicated as necessary additions to the *Dutch Catechism* was 'the doctrine on the experience of angels, which is based on the Gospel and on the Tradition of the church' (AAS 1968, p.685).

22. *Catechism of the Council of Trent*, part I, commentary on the Creed, c. ii, n.5.

In the Our Father, the word 'heaven' includes the world of the angels. Thus when—this catechism says—we pray God that his will be done on earth as it is in heaven, we are asking that 'our conformity to the will of God be regulated according to the rule observed in heaven by the blessed angels and choirs of heavenly spirits, that, as they willingly and with supreme joy obey God, we too may yield a cheerful obedience to his will in the manner most acceptable to him' (*Catechism of the Council of Trent for Parish Priests*, trs. McHugh and Callan, p. 537).

By exhorting us to pray that the will of God be done 'on earth as it is in heaven', Christ asks that 'the will of God be done by men as it is done by angels', to use St Augustine's phrase. The Master is proposing the angels to us as models (*De Serm. Domini in Monte*, Book III, c. 6, quoted by Raissa Maritain, *Notes sur le Pater*, Paris 1962, p. 17).

23. St Thomas distinguished 'providence' (reason in the planned disposition of things) and the disposing and execution, which is termed 'government' (*Summa Theologiae*, I, q. 22, a.1, ad 2): providence is exclusive to God whereas in government he involves men and angels.

24. The text is included in *Il dono della air chiarezza* (addresses etc by Albino Luciani, as bishop and as pope), Rome 1979, pp. 125-159).

25. Op. cit., p. 146.

IN THE BIBLE AND THE LITURGY

1. To avoid any ambiguity, we would point out that the word 'angel' (meaning 'envoy') is used in five different senses in sacred Scripture. It is applied to the Word, sent by the Father to the world; to St John the Baptist, the

Precursor; to priests, who are as it were God's ambassadors to the people; to prophets, who foretell the future, speaking in God's name; and, finally, to angels properly so called, heavenly spirits sent by God to men. The term is generally used in this last sense.

2. Cf. *Bulletin du cercle thomiste Sainte-Nicolas*, May 1965, p. 50.

3. Cf. *Présence et prophetie*, Fribourg 1942, p. 258.

4. When pursuing the English troops in Beauce, Joan of Arc cried, 'Even if they were suspended from the clouds, they would be ours'; Paul Doncoeur, *Paroles et lettres de Jeanne la Pucelle*, Paris 1960, p. 73.

5. This is Cornelius a Lapide's interpretation; he cites a similar angelic apparition in the life of St Francis Xavier, before he left for India (*Commentaire des Actes des Apotres* 16:9).

6. Anton Haenggi and Irmgard Pahl, *Prex eucharistica, textus e variis liturgiis antiquioribus selecti*, Fribourg 1968, p. 341.

7. *Memorial*, I April 1543 (*Collection Christus*, No. 4, Paris 1959, p. 325).

8. In Theodor Bogler, *Die Engel in der Welt von heute*, Maria Laach, 1960, p.11.

9. 'When God approaches men, when he comes from heaven, that is, from that higher part of Creation, towards earth, he is accompanied by or he comes with his angels who dispense his largesse and who are the ministers of his watchfulness and solicitude towards us:' J. Bosc, *Anges, demons et etres intermediaires*, Paris 1968, p.199.

HERE BELOW WE WILL NEVER KNOW

1. *Quaestiones quodlibetales*, III, q.3, a.7.

2. *Summa Theologiae*, I, q.50, a.2.

3. Fifth homily against the Anomoeans.

4. First sermon on the feast of St Michael.

5. *De consideratione*, Book V, c.IV.

6. *Sermons de Tauler*, ed. Hugueny, Théry and Corin, Vol. III, Paris 1927, pp. 129-130.

7. *Nostro Tempo*, Turin, 22 October 1967.

8. Paul VI, Address at general audience, 12 June 1968.

9. Ibid., 30 October 1968.

10. Ibid., 31 May 1967.

11. Cardinal Renard, interview, *La Croix*, 30 June 1967.

12. Paul VI, Address at general audience, 14 June 1967.

13. Diminutives used in some languages to designate the guardian angel are certainly not suited to inspire respect: cf. in Italian: 'angelino custode'.

14. It would be extremist in the other direction to forbid Christian piety the use of all forms of imagery of angels. 'What the devil was doing with the Lutherans,' wrote St Teresa of Avila, 'was taking from them all means of awakening greater love' such as religious images: Relation XXX in *Complete Works*, ed. Peers, vol. I, London 1946, p. 349.

15. St Thomas points out a difference between Zechariah and the Virgin Mary, to both of whom the Archangel Gabriel appears: 'Zechariah was troubled when he saw him, and fear fell upon him' (Lk 1:12), whereas Mary 'was

greatly troubled at the saying (at what Gabriel said), and considered in her mind what sort of greeting this might be' (Lk 1:20). Some people, St Thomas comments, 'claim that since the blessed Virgin was accustomed to seeing angels she was not bothered much at the sight of this one. The words he spoke caused the disturbance, for she wondered at them, not thinking herself as great as all that. For this reason Scripture says she was deeply disturbed not at seeing the angel but "at his words"'; *Summa Theologiae*, III, q. 30, a. 3, ad. 3.

16. *Les images*, Fribourg 1950, pp. 28-29.

17. Joseph Duhr, 'Anges' in *Dictionnaire de spiritualité*, vol. 1, Paris 1937, col. 621.

18 *Summa Theologiae*, supl. q.76, a. 3. Commentaries on the Epistles of St Paul, *ad Eph.* 1:21. 'In the Apocalypse some angels appear as being in charge of natural phenomena,' Cardinal Journet wrote (*L'Eglise du Verbe Incarné*, vol. III, Paris 1962, p. 237), citing Origen, *In Jerem.*, hom. X, n. 6; PG 13, col. 365; and St Augustine, *De genesi ad litteram*, Book VIII, chap. 23, n.44. But, he went on to point out, 'this angelic action, as also that deriving from our freedom, can occur without in any way undermining the laws of the universe.'

19. Twelfth homily on the Psalm *Qui habitat*.

20. Blessed J. Escrivá, *The Way*, Dublin 1981, no. 566.

21. *Enarr. in Ps 103*, sermon 1, 15.

22. Cf. R. Vancourt in *France Catholique*, 10 March 1967: '*Satan existe-t-il?*'

23. *Summa Theologiae*, II-II, q.13, a.1.

24. Address, 30 October 1968. The pope added: 'Left to private initative, study of the Bible leads to such a variety of opinions that subjective certainty of faith is disturbed and faith is despoiled of its social authority. The result is that faith of this type undermines unity among believers whereas it ought to be the very basis of agreement of thoughts and minds: "there is but one faith"' (Eph 4:5). These words of Paul VI are not a general condemnation of modern biblical studies as some have tried to make out. What the pope rejects is exegesis which is blind to the light of Tradition and of the Magisterium. 'It is clear that sacred tradition, sacred Scripture, and the teaching authority of the Church, in accord with God's most wise design, are so linked and joined together that one cannot stand without the others, and that all together and each in its own way under the action of the one Holy Spirit contribute effectively to the salvation of souls' (Vatican II, Dogmatic Constitution *Dei Verbum*, no. 10).

25. *Summa Theologiae*, I, q.113, a.7 and 8.

26. Ibid., I, q.110.

27. Cf. *Commentary on the sentences* II, dist. 10, a.2 ad 2, etc.

28. *Summa Theologiae*, I, q.112, a.2, ad. 2.

29. On the controversial subject of the Angel of Yahweh, cf. Auvray, 'L'Ange dans le Bible' in the encyclopedia *Catholicisme*, vol. I col. 539.

30. Paul VI, *Creed of the People of God*.

CRACKS AND AMBUSHES

1. *Summa Theologiae*, I, q.113, a.1, ad. 1.

2. Ibid., I-II, q.85, a.3. In his address to the general audience on 12 April 1971, Paul VI refers to 'certain incurable effects of Original Sin'.

3. R. Bernard, *Commentaire de la Somme théologique*, 'Le peché', vol. II, Paris 1931, p.303.

4. Blessed J. Escrivá, *Christ is passing by*, Dublin 1982, No. 63.

5. Sermon for the feast of the Guardian Angels, *Oeuvres oratoires de Bossuet*, ed. Lebarq, vol. III, p. 105.

6. *This we believe*, Shannon 1969, p. 160.

7. Ibid., pp. 141f.

8. Twelfth sermon, on the Psalm *Qui habitat*.

9. Cf. *Summa theologiae*, Supl., 89, 8, ad 2.

10. Cf II *Commentary on the sentences* dist. 6, q.1, a.5, ad. 4.

11. Ibid., dist. 6, q.1, a.3.

12. Cf. *Summa Theologiae*, I, q.64, a.4.

13. C.V. Heris, 'Les anges' in *Somme Théologique*, Paris 1953, p. 431.

14. *Enarr. in Ps.*, Ps 8: *Potestas ista est sub potestate*.

15. In a poignant page of *L'Imposture* George Bernanos describes the devil's power over man's faculties and the limits he meets in the form of the inviolablity of the will and, especially, the power of grace.
'Despite the enemy's subtlety, his most ingenious malice cannot penetrate the soul except indirectly, in the way a city can be forced by poisoning its water supply. He deceives one's judgement, entices one's imagination, stirs one's blood, with infinite skill turns to his use the contradictions we meet, confounds our joys, deepens our sorrows, vitiates our actions and intentions deep down: yet even then he has not managed to destroy us. He must obtain, from ourselves, our full consent. And this he will not get until God has had his turn to speak. No matter how much he wants to keep divine grace at bay, grace must bloom: the enemy awaits this growth with terror, for it means that his patient work may be destroyed in an instant. He has no idea where the ray of grace will strike.'

16. C. Sauve, *L'Ange intime*, p. 108.

17. Mgr. Gay, *Sermons*, II, pp. 22-23.

18. Pietro Rossano, *Meditazioni su San Paolo*, vol. I, Rome 1967, p. 621.

19. *Summa Theologiae*, II-II, q.176, a.6.

20. C.D. Boulogne, *Le monde des spirits*, Paris 1945, p. 141.

21. Cf. St Thomas, *Commentary on the Book of Job*, c.40 and 41.

22. Cf. *Sermons de Tauler*, ed. Hugueny and others, Paris 1927, vol. III, pp. 132-133.

23. Talk given to the Daughters of Charity (1640) in *Correspondence et entretiens*, vol. IX, p. 32.

24. Nil de St Brocard, 'Demonio e vita spirituale' in *Sanjuanistica*, Rome 1943, p. 163.

25. Wilhelm Vischer, *Das Christus zeugnis des Altens Testaments*, p. 112, quoted by H. Christmann, in *Summa theologica, deutschlateinische Ausgabe, Vol. 8: Erhaltung und Regierung der Welt*, Heidelberg-Munchen, 1951, p. 358.

26. H. Christmann, loc. cit.

27. L. Bouyer, *Le mystère pascal*, quoted by Cardinal Garrone in *This we believe*, Shannon 1969, p. 147.

28. PL 74, 278 quoted in J. Duhr, *Dictionnaire de spiritualité*, col. 590.

29. Homily for Ascension Day.

30. I, q.114, a.1, ad. 2.

31. A reference to the episode reported in 2 Kings 6:15ff: Gehazi, Elisha's servant, is in despair, seeing the city of Dothan surrounded by enemy troops come to seize his master. Elisha prays 'Lord, open his eyes that he may see'. The Lord does so and Gehazi saw 'the mountain full of horses and chariots of fire'. Then the enemy was struck with blindness.

32. Johannes Brinktrine, *Die Lehre von der Schopfung*, Paderborn 1956, p. 175.

33. Cf. *Satan*, collective work published by *Etudes carmelitaines*, Paris, 1948, pp. 640-643.

34. Jn 8 :40.

35. Jean Guitton, 'Introduction' to Hedwige Louis Chevrillon, *Le prince du mensonge*, Paris 1970, pp. 9-10.

36. Cardinal Faulhaber, *Zeitrufe, Gottesrufe*, Freiburg i.Br., 1933, pp. 416-429.

TO GUARD YOU IN ALL YOUR WAYS

1. Romano Guardini, *Der Engel des Menschen*.

2. *Summa Theologiae*, I, q.113, a.4, ad 3.

4. *Summa Theologiae*, II-II, q.68, a.1, ad 1.

5. *Le monde des esprits*, p. 165. At a conference organised in 1968 on the subject of angels, devils and intermediary beings, Cardinal Danièlou stressed the role of good and bad angels in artistic inspiration. 'Artistic creation has . . . angelic characteristics. This also explains its extraordinary ambiguity. Its beauty is fascinating but there is the danger that it may become the object of a kind of idolatry. This is what directly relates the sphere of art to that other sphere of angelology and of demonology. When Gide says that there is no work of art in which the devil does not take part, he is saying something which in my opinion is perfectly correct, but I would add "in which devil *or angel* does not take part." In other words, Gide's mistake lies in not recognizing that art contains, first and foremost, our angelic aspects' (*Anges, démons et etres intermediairies*, Paris, 1969, p. 45).

6. Declaration *Nostra Aetate*, on relations with non-Christian religions, no. 2. 'According to St John's gospel (1:9) God "enlightens every man" and St Paul says (Acts 14:17) that God "did not leave himself without witness". In his speech in the Arcopagus, Paul exclaims: "What therefore you worship as unknown, this I proclaim to you" (Acts 17:23). The Church has always been ready to recognize and honour "holy pagans" whom the Old Testament presents to us and whom we have just listed (Abel, Enoch, Daniel, Noah, Melchizedek, Lot, the Queen of Sheba). Everywhere and in all periods there are people who believe in Christ without knowing him and who "invisibly" belong to the "visible church"' (C. Journet, *L'Eglise du Verbe incarné*, vol. 1, Paris 1941, p. 46). Non-Christian religions, in the Vedas and the Upanishads, in Buddha and Lao-Tse, do contain truths, and in Buddhism and other

religions there are very fine moral ideas. If St Justin placed Socrates and other pagans among the saints, they can also include, as Danièlou says, other great figures of pagan religion, Zoroaster and Buddha (*Les saints 'paiens'de l'Ancient testament*, p. 29).

Thomas Ohm in *Faites des disciples de toutes les nations* (Paris, vol. III, pp. 48-52) observes that Christians' views of natural religions include a wide range of opinions from radical condemnation (à la Karl Barth) to the naive approach of some Christians who give up their faith and actually join some eastern religions.

Vatican II avoids both extremes: natural religions are neither totally bad nor totally good; they contain truths intermixed with errors.

7. *De Veritate*, q.14, a.11, ad. 1.

8. Cf. *Summa Theologiae*, I, q.III, a.4.

9. St Robert Bellarmine, *Commentary on the Psalms*: Psalm 90.

10. Although they operate in a wide variety of ways, most of guardian angels' efforts are spent in enlightening men's minds (cf. *Summa Theologiae*, I, q.113, a.1, ad. 2 and a.6 ad. 2).

11. *The Way*, Dublin 1981, No. 565.

12. Cf. *Summa Theologiae*, II-II, q. 113, a.1.

13. Cf. AAS 1962, p. 792.

14. This truth was repeatedly affirmed by Paul VI, especially in his addresses to theologians (cf. address of 6 October 1969 to the International Theological Commission: AAS 1969, pp. 713-716).

15. Cf. *Summa Theologiae*, I, q.113, a.5, ad. 2.

16. Ibid., I, q.111.

17. St Thomas liked to ackwledge what he owed to 'the intellectual assistance of angels' (cf. C.D. Boulogne, *Le monde des esprits*, p. 170).

18. II *Commentary on the Sentences*, dist. 11, q.1, ad. 6.

19. An endless river of sense-images flows through us; these the angels work on, thrusting into the background those which are gross, unhealthy or useless and emphasizing those which are more refined, correct and healthy. These images they reinforce and in doing so make them clearer and more noble. Usually we do not realize any of this is going on. Whether on the good or the evil side, the action on us of a pure spirit is essentially discreet: the devil's, out of shrewdness; the angel's, out of discretion (. . .). Inside our imagination the angel cleanses our images; he enriches our thinking by moving our ideas: He helps us without drawing attention to himself. Similarly in our search for the truth, we are often unaware of the part played by our angel. Who can say how our thoughts arise, who can plumb the complex, mysterious chemistry of the human spirit?: C.D. Boulogne, op. cit., pp. 161-167.

20. *Summa Theologiae*, I, q.11, a.1. 'Intellectus humanus . . . fortificatur per actionem intellectus angelici'. Cf. *De Veritate*, XI, 3 ad 12; *Quod lib.* 9, a.10 ad. 3.

21. *Journal spirituel de Lucie-Christine* (1870-1908), 6 October 1883, Paris 1938, p. 173.

22. A. Arrighini, *Gli Angeli buoni e cattivi*, Rome, 1937, p. 431. Grandmaison

describes the radiance of friends of God: 'it is a recognized fact that pure souls emit a radiation; that they inspire good thoughts keep evil thoughts away, act in some way like a "sacrament" (saving, of course, grace *ex opere operato*, which is on another level). "God is here": one senses this in the presence of a Stanislaus Kostka, John Berchmans, Louis Gonzaga, Rose of Lima, Catherine of Siena. Children and sinners (the latter if touched by grace) feel this influence particularly, because they are in tune with pure souls (or out of tune with them, and therefore feel the need for being in tune): hence the attraction, devotion to the Blessed Virgin holds for many people and so many sinners *Ecrits spirituels*, I, Conférence, p. 20.

23. J. Legrand, *L'Universe et l'homme dans la philosophie de saint Thomas*, vol. II, Paris 1946, p. 63.

24. *Summa contra gentiles*, III, c.92.

25. J. Legrand, op. cit., pp. 60-61.

26. Cf. *Summa Theologiae*, I, q.111, a.1, ad. 3.

27. *The Spiritual Exercises*, trs. Thomas Corbishley, SJ, London 1963, p. 113.

28. Etienne Souriau, one-time teacher at the Sorbonne suggests there is scope for research into mysterious intervention in our lives by beings intermediary between God and men. 'Everyone can say, "On such and such a day, at such a time, in such and such circumstances, I had the sensation of receiving a kind of message which enlightened me and orientated me": everyone has positive experience to offer in this regard. Along the same lines, I have felt that one could speak in connection with artistic creation, of an intervention of what I might call the "angel of the work of art", an energy which awakens the artist in the middle of the night to get him to think about the symphony he is working on, the as yet unfinished statue, the play still in outline, and which forces him to think that the finishing and total perfection of that work of art are for them a matter of the utmost importance' (paper at colloquium on *Anges, démons et êtres intermediares*, pp. 32-33). Souriau here is speaking as a psychologist, without reference to the data of Revelation. He confided to Jean Guitton that he had 'experience of propitious intermediary beings, who are guides to us as individuals and also to the groupings to which we belong.'

29. *Memorie biografiche*, II. 264.

30. 'God is not a jeweller, a watchmaker, a manufacturer of natures. The world is not a watch, it is a republic of natures' (Jacques Maritain, *Raison et raisons*, p. 62).

31. Cf. *Summa Theologiae*, I, q.113, a.1 ad. 2.

32. Ibid., I, q.111, a.2, ad. 2.

33. 'The Holy Spirit does not always inspire us directly. Sometimes he uses the guardian angel, a preacher, a good book, a friend; but it is always he in the last analysis who is the principal author of that inspiration' (Antonio Royo Marin, *El gran desconocido: El Espiritu santo y sus dones*, Madrid 1971, p. 211).

34. Fifth sermon on the angels.

35. Eleventh sermon on the Psalm *Qui habitat*.

36. Zac 1:14.

37. *De consideratione*, 1. 5, c.5.

38. *Spiritual canticle* chap. XXV, in *The Complete Works of St John of the Cross*, ed., E. Allison Peers, vol. II, London, 1943, p. 162.

39. Ibid., p. 161 and 162.

40. *Summa Theologiae*, II-II, q.172, a.2, ad. 2.

41. He called him 'my childhood companion', according to Fr Eusebio da Castelpetroso.

42. Ennemond Boniface, *Thérèse Newman—la stigmatistée*, Paris 1956, p. 169.

43. Ibid., p. 174.

44. One day I asked Alexandra, the six-year-old daughter of two doctors, both of them have a very strong faith, (the family were on holiday in the mountains): 'Does your guardian angel also take holidays?' 'Oh no', she said, 'he is always at my side because if he left me, then I would be bold . . .'

45. *The Angels and their Mission*, Westminster 1957, p. 63.

46. Ibid., p. 64.

47. Fourth homily on the incomprehensibility of God.

48. *Ele sentido teológica de la liturgiá*, Madrid 1965, p. 334.

49. *Recherches sur le Notre Pere*, Paris, 1969, pp. 112-133 and 397 'Despite the authority of this Catechism', he adds, 'this recomendation is little more than a dead letter among Catholics'. (p. 113).

50. *Summa Theologiae*, III, q.8 a.4, c.

51. Ibid, III, q.8, a 6, ad. 2.

52. *Treatise on the priesthood*, VI, 4.

53. *Commentary on the Epistles of St Paul*, ad. 1 Cor 11: 10.

54. In this connection Blessed J. Escrivá says: 'I adore and praise with the angels—it is not difficult, because I know that, as I celebrate the holy Mass, they surround me, adoring the Blessed Trinity: *Christ is passing by*, Dublin 1982, no. 89.

55. *De oratione*, 31, 5.

56. *Dialogues*, IV, 58.

57. Cfr. 1 Cor 11:10. One of the main witnesses at the process of beatification of Theresa of the Child Jesus, Mother Agnes of Jesus, various times Prioress of the Lisieux Carmel, referred to the refinement and vigilance of the saints in things to do with chastity: 'When she was alone she in no way neglected modesty, for the reason that she was in the presence of angels': this is reminiscent of St Paul's advice and how it might be applied in everyday life: *Procès de beatification et canonisation de sainte Thérèse de l'Enfant-Jesus et de la Sainte-Face, I: Procés informatif ordinaire*, published by Teresianum, Rome, 1973, p. 170.

58. *Stromata* VII, 12.

59. *De oratione*, 16.

60. In his Epistle 219, Alcuin reports an amusing episode from the life of St Bede, Doctor of the Church: 'It is told of Bede that he used to say: "I know that the angels come at the canonical hours: . . . what would happen if they were not to find me with my brothers? Would they not ask; "Where, then, is Bede?"'

61. *Hom. in Luc.*, 23.

62. *Sermon for the feast of the Guardian Angels*, point two, ed. Lebarq, vol. 3, pp. 108-109.

63. Cf. *Summa Theologiae*, I, q.114, a.3, ad. 2.

THEY SEE GOD

1. Cf. *Summa theologiae*, I, q.113, a.7. Royo Marín comments on St Thomas follows: 'The guardian angels do not suffer on account of *physical* evils which affect their protegés (illnesses, sorrows, persecution, etc), because they know that 'in everything God works for good with those who love him (Rom 8:28). Nor do they suffer an account of men's sins, because God allows these to occur in order to draw out greater good (through later repentance and penance). Nor do they suffer on account of the eternal condemnation of their protegis, just as the blessed in heaven will not suffer when they see some relative of theirs in hell (cf. *Supl.* 94, 2). The reason is because they are in no way to blame for the condemnation of those souls—they did everything they could to avoid it, by inspiring them, giving them good advice, protecting them from countless dangers, etc.—and only the sinner's rebellion is the cause of their eternal loss. Once sinners are confirmed in evil and definitively fixed in sin the angels desire is to see divine justice done: this means inexorable punishment (though less than they deserve, according to the Angelic Doctor) and by the same token the angels feel no pain of sadness at their eternal condemnation' (*Dios y su obra*, Madrid, 1963, pp. 411-412).

2. Cf. *Summa Theologiae*, I, q.113, a.7 c.

3. Radio message, 29 June 1941.

4. Cf. *Summa Theologiae*, Supl., q.72, a.1 ad. 1. It is important to differentiate clearly betweeen the will of God, in the sense of commandment, and the will of God in the sense of disposition or plan. The first proscribes every moral fault, whereas the second includes the good and bad done by men. Here on earth many things are done which are against the will-commandment of God, but nothing happens that is outside his will-design. Providence embraces and uses everything in a mysterious way to achieve its ends: 'all things are your servants' (Ps 119, 91).

5. Cf. J. Duhr, 'Anges' in *Dictionnaire de Spiritualité*.

6. *Spiritual Canticle*, chap. XXIX (trs. Peers), op. cit., p. 149f.

7. Enchiridion, c.27.

8. *Quartre mystiques anglais*, Paris 1942, p. 84; the reference to Julian is *Revelations of Divine Love*, ed. Roger Hudleston, London 1952, ch. 27, p. 48.

9. II *Commentary on the Sentences*, dist. 10, q.1, a.4.

10. 2 *Moral.*, c.3.

11. Cf. *Summa Theologiae*, I, q.112, a.1, ad. 3.

12 Cf. *Commentaries of St Thomas on the Gospel of St John*, ad. 15.5.

13. The Venerable Francis Libermann, first superior general of the Holy Ghost Fathers, letter to a superior, 28 September 1836 in *Lettres spirituelles*, vol. I, p. 203.

14. *Journal spirituel de Lucie-Christine*, 21 February 1884.

15. Letter to her uncle, 1 March 1909.

16. Letter to her spiritual director, 15 May 1911.
17. Quoted in M.T. Guignet, *Une expérience mystique, Marie Antoinette de Geuser*, Paris, 1941, p. 112.
18. Address, 24 April 1957.
19. Dom García M. Colombas monk of Montserrat Abbey, *Paradis et vie angélique*, Paris 1961, p. 11.
20. Cf. Mass of St Louis Gonzaga.
21. Cf. Daniel-Rops, *The Church in the Seventeenth Century*, trs. J.J. Buckingham, vol. 1, New York 1965, p. 32.
22. Marie-Eugéne de l'Enfant Jésus, OCD, *Je veux voir Dieu*, Tarrascon 1956, pp. 1071f.

SITTING AT HIS GATE
1. *The Way*, op. cit. No. 562.
2. Commentary on the Epistle to the Romans, ad. 1:10.
3. Commentary on St Matthew, ad. 4, 11.
4. Fifth sermon the angels.
5. II *Commentary on the Sentences*, dist. 7, q.2, art. 2, ad. 5.
6. Eleventh sermon on the psalm *Qui habitat*.
7. First sermon for the feast of St Michael.
8. *Memorial* 15 June 1545, Paris 1959, p. 138. Paul VI observed 'when consciences lose their hold on the meaning of chastity, one can notice also a lessening of their capacity to accept the word of God, to desire eternal life, to thirst after conversation with God': Jean Guitton, *Dialogues avec Paul VI*, Paris 1967, p. 332.
9. Third sermon on the Epiphany.
10. *Opuscules de piété, p. 119.*
11. Cf. St Thomas, *Compendium theologiae*, 2nd pt., c.2.
12. In this creation, effected by God himself, of dispositions necessary for responding to grace, may lie the solution of a problem posed by the philosopher Henri Bergson, in connection with radical, instantaneous conversion such as that of St Paul on the road to Damascus. 'In order to correctly understand the nature of these radical changes in conscience,' he said one day to Jean Guitton, 'one would love to study similar phenomena today. I know of one, which my friend William James told me about. It had to do with a person who was hostile to Catholicism, a person called Ratisbonne. At one in the afternoon, Ratisbonne, out of politeness, entered some particular church in Rome. At ten past one Ratisbonne came out, utterly and definitively changed, absolutely convinced. How can we explain instanteous and permanent changes of this type? This is the problem.' Jean Guitton recalled these reflections of his old teacher Bergson in connection with the publication of *Dieu existe, je l'ai rencontre* by André Frossard: cf. 'Une mutation instantanée' in *Le Figaro*, 14 February 1969.
13. *Summa Theologiae*, II-II, q.172, a.3. This article discusses whether the charism of prophecy necessarily calls for natural dispositions in the prophet.
14. God's love for us totally exceeds our ability to grasp it. As St Thomas puts

it: 'The measure and rule of our faith is God's truth: of our charity, God's goodness; of our hope, his sheer omnipotence and mercy. This measure surpasses all human power, so that never can we love God as much as he ought to be loved, nor believe and hope in him as much as we should. Much less, therefore, can there be excess here': *Summa Theologiae*, I-II, q. 64, a. 4. And the holy angels are one of the main channels through which God's abundant favours reach men.

LOOKING TO THE FUTURE

1. *The peasant of the Caronne*, London 1968, p. 53.

2. Address, 7 December 1968.

3. We might quote these lines written before World War Two by a person who seems to have been on intimate terms with the angels: 'The devil is astute; he is at present working on future priests to bring about a relaxation of faith and morals. The existence of angels will be attacked; devotion to the Blessed Virgin will be viewed as sentimentalism ... even priests, university professors and teachers of religion will describe devotion to Our Lady and the saints as an exaggeration and will encourage the faithful instead to address God directly and have no longer this childish recourse to the saints': Mechtilde Thaller, *Journal* published by Friedrich Ritter von Rama (Ein Buchlein von den Engeln), French trans., Switzerland 1971.

At the end of his study of theology of angels, Georges Tavard asks why there has been a decline in devotion to angels. A significant cause, he feels, is lack of interest on theologians' part ever since the Middle Ages. Theologians tend to deal with subjects which interest their contemporaries: but this tendency allows rationalism and naturalism to seep into the Christian fold. Other causes he suggests are the laity being 'turned off' by the odd language of the liturgy (until the recent reform) and modern skepticism towards theses on angels which are not based directly on Revelation. He sees liturgical reform as leading to a new growth in devotion to angels—and points to Vatican II's confirmation of traditional doctrine as also favouring same. Michael Schmaus, Alois Grillmeier and Leo Scheffczyk, *Handbuch der Dogmengeschichte*, vol, II, fasc. 2b: *Die Engel*, by Georges Tavard, with A. Caquot and J. Michl, 1968, pp. 95-96.

4. At Maria Laach (1957), Mont Saint-Michel (1967) and Paris 1968.

5. Address, 27 February 1966, in St Pancras' Basilica.

6. In 1969-70, a survey taking in the views of 22,000 priests indicated that many of them suffered from loneliness.

7. Jean Calvet, *La lumière de complies*, pp. 215-216. 'I received a severe lesson' he adds. 'The Christian people uphold traditions while intellectuals abandon them. Contrary to what we sometimes might think, we do not lose contact with our sources; they are still there, but deeper in the subsoil.'

8. Cf. *Journal spirituel*, 16, June 1903.

9. *Summa Theologiae*, I, q.109, a.4.

10. Ibid., I, q.112, a.l, ad,4.

11. Paul Doncoeur, op. cit., p. 60.

12. Duhr, art. cit.

13. *Le soulier de satin*, day 1, scene 12.

14. Address, 29 September 1967.

15. *Carnet de notes*, Paris 1960, p.363.

16. *El sentido teológico de la liturgia*, Madrid 1965, p. 330.

17. H. de Lubac, *Sur les chemins de Dieu*, Paris 1956, p. 112.

18. Paul Doncoeur, op. cit.

19. Sermon at St Mary's, 16 July 1837, on the invisible world.

20. *Présence et prophétie*, second note on the angels, pp. 261-262.

21. Lavy, *Les Anges*, Paris 1890, p. 51.

22. *Livre des visions et instructions*, chap. 38.

23. Germano, *Santa Gemma Galgani*, pp. 209-210. A contemporary, non-Christian poet, Rainer Maria Rilke, has an intuition of the angels' super-human splendour in his *Duino Elegies*.

24. Op. cit., 207.

25. *The Angels and their Mission*, p. viii.

26. *Summa Theologiae*, II, q.110, a.1.

27. *The Angels and their Mission*, p.4.

28. *L'Eglise du Verbe incarné*, vol. III, Paris 1969, p. 236.

29. *Parochial and Plain Sermons*, vol. II, London 1891, p. 362: Sermon on 'The Powers of Nature'.

30. Ibid., passim.

31. *Les anges au ciel et parmi nous*, p. 95.

32. Lavy, *Les Anges*, pp. 185-186.

33. Cf. Paul VI, Address, 24 February 1966. He develops these thoughts in his address on Christmas night 1968 to steelworkers of Tarento: Technology harnesses the laws of nature: 'But these laws are nothing other than thoughts: thoughts hidden in things, imperative thoughts which not only give things the names we normally use such as iron, fire, etc, but a particular being which the things (obviously) cannot give themselves: a received being, a being which we call received. In each phase of your work you are encountering this created being, that is, this being that is thought. Thought by whom? Without realizing it, you are extracting from things a reply, a word, a law, a thought which lives in things. If we think about it well, this thought reveals to us the hand, the power, what shall we say?, the presence, immanent and transcendent—that is to say, a presence within it and above it—of a thinking, almighty Spirit, to whom we are accustomed to give the name which now rises to our trembling lips, the mysterious name of God': *Osservatore Romano*, 27 December 1968.

Index of authors

Alcuin, 122
Ambrose, St, 53
Angela of Foligno, 108
Angelini, C., 102
Aristotle, 10
Arrighini, A., 120
Augustine, St, 10, 11, 41, 48, 86, 103, 117
Auvray, P., 117

Bergson, H., 124
Bellamine, St Robert, 25, 120
Benedict, St, 77f
Bernard, R., 118
Bernard, St, 14, 34, 40, 47, 50, 71
Bernanos, G., 118
Berulle, P., 97
Bolger, T., 116
Bonaventure, St, 70f, 96
Boniface, E., 122
Bosc, J., 116
Bosco, St John, 68
Bossuet, 45f, 79
Boulogne, C.D., 49, 58, 118, 120
Bouttier, M., 9
Bouyer, L., 51
Brinktrine, J., 119

Calvert, J., 102f
Canisius, St Peter, 114
Carmignac, J., 76
Capovilla, L., 20
Christmann, H., 118
Claudel, P., 24, 106, 107
Clement of Alexandria, St, 78
Columbas, G.M., 124
Confalonieri, C., 15, 114
Cornelius a Lapide, 116

Cyril of Alexandria, St, 32
Danièlou, J., 19, 74f, 109, 119
Daniel-Rops, H., 124
Doncoeur, P., 116
Duhr, J., 117, 123, 126

Escrivá, Blessed J., 40, 45, 61, 92, 122

Faber, St Peter, 32f, 97
Faulhaber, 56
Francis de Sales, St, 20, 67, 105
Frossard, A., 124

Garrone, G.M., 12, 46, 47
Gay, C.L., 118
Germano, C.P., 128
Geuser, M.A. de 89
Gide, A., 119
Grandmaison, L., 120
Gregory the Great, St, 24, 77, 88
Guardini, R., 57
Guitton, J., 55f, 119, 121

Haenggi, A., 116
Heris, C.V., 118
Hildebrand, D. von, 100

Ignatius Loyola, St, 66, 84, 90
John XXIII, 13, 14, 18f, 23, 34, 39, 62, 67

John Chrysostom, St, 8, 34f, 53, 75, 76f
John of the Cross, St, 51, 71, 85f
John Paul I, 22
Journet, C., 8ff, 38, 92, 109, 119
Julian of Norwich, 86